Rudolph Etzenhouser

The Book Unsealed

An exposition of prophecy and American antiquities, the claims of the

Book of Mormon, examined and sustained

Rudolph Etzenhouser

The Book Unsealed

An exposition of prophecy and American antiquities, the claims of the Book of Mormon, examined and sustained

ISBN/EAN: 9783337298975

Printed in Europe, USA, Canada, Australia, Japan

Cover: Foto ©Lupo / pixelio.de

More available books at **www.hansebooks.com**

THE
Book Unsealed.

AN

Exposition of Prophecy

AND

AMERICAN ANTIQUITIES.

The Claims of the Book of Mormon Examined and Sustained.

"As I have thought,
So shall it stand;
As I have purposed,
So shall it come to pass."
—Jehovah.

By ELDER R. ETZENHOUSER,

OF THE

Reorganized Church of Jesus Christ of Latter Day Saints.

Independence, Mo.
ENSIGN PRINT.
1892.

PREFACE.

The author of this little work makes no claim to scholarship in the presentation of its pages, and prefers that it shall be judged by the measure of truth it contains, rather than by its quality as a literary production.

For years past he has waited patiently, hoping that some of the "household of faith" would recognize the necessity for such publication, and supply the demand for a work of this kind; but none so far has appeared.

Under the solicitations and encouragement of kind friends, he now essays to present a brief exposition of the subject, leaving for abler pens, the preparation of more elaborate and exhaustive work.

He has endeavored to furnish a compact array of evidences clearly and tersely; so that it may prove itself a helper to the "defender of the faith," and a blessing unto the seeker after truth.

Just the degree of success he has attained in his efforts, if indeed any at all, remains for the future and the candid public to determine.

Matter contributed and aid rendered by Elder T. E. Lloyd of Independence, Mo., is most cheerfully acknowledged.

With the desire that the cause of truth may be promoted, and that through the blessing of God, it may be the means of bringing some to the knowledge of the great Latter Day Work, these pages are respectfully submitted   R. E.

INDEPENDENCE, Mo., May 25, 1892.

Table of Contents.

CHAPTER 1.—The Book of Mormon.
" 2.—Continents and Nations.
" 3.—The Jaredites from Babel.
" 4.—Two Distinct and Highly Civilized People.
" 5.—Books, Weaving and Dyeing.
" 6.—Israel in America.
" 7.—Hebrew Relics, Customs and Languages in America.
" 8.—Egyptian Resemblances and Language in America.
" 9.—Plates—Records.
" 10.—Metals, Tools, Implements and Instruments.
" 11.—Dates of American Antiquities. When Published.
" 12.—Joseph Smith's Object—A Vision.
" 13.—The Sealed Book to come forth. Fulfillment of Ps. 85 and Isa. 29. Palestine Restored.
" 14.—An admission. Witnesses testify.
" 15.—Conclusions

CHAPTER I.
THE BOOK OF MORMON.

The Book of Mormon derives its name from the writer of one of the several books of which it is composed, whose name was Mormon, and who compiled the several books as they appear. The book, by those not acquainted with it, has been supposed to countenance and sanction the institution of polygamy, while just the opposite is true; nothing in the realm of literature being more condemnatory of polygamy.

"Wherefore, my brethren, hear me, and hearken to the word of the Lord: For there shall not any man among you have save it be one wife: and concubines he shall have none, for I the Lord God delighteth in the chastity of women."—Book of Mormon, page 116; N. E., page 102, verse 29.

The time the book of Mormon covers is divided into two periods; the first, from the confusion of languages at Babel, from whence the first colony, the Jaredites came to the western continent, to the time they became extinct, which was wrought through a series of bloody wars before the Nephite colony came over from Jerusalem, which migration occurred during the reign of Zedekiah, king of Judah, about 600 B. C. This colony having become possessed of the Jaredite record, and having completed their own, added the record of the former people in an abridged form.

The second colony, some years after their arrival here, divided, each party taking the name of its respective leader, and so were known as Nephites and Lamanites.

The Jaredites, like the Nephites and Lamanites, were of the white race. The Lamanites because of their rebellion against God and his appointments, were cursed with a dark or copper colored skin, their descendants being the American Indians of to-day. Both of the colonies were a highly civilized, enlightened and religious people, and attained excellence in art, science, architecture and agriculture.

The Nephites lost their national existence in war with the Lamanites about the year 420 of the Christian era; the remnant of that people were then merged into the Lamanites. Their records were hidden in the place from which they were taken in 1827 by Joseph Smith, the translator of the book.

CHAPTER II.
CONTINENTS AND NATIONS.

There being two continents, nothing is more reasonable than that the people of each may have had recognition from, and communication with God

That this is clearly admissible, is evident from Acts 17: 24-27. "God that hath made the world, and all things * * hath made of one blood all nations of men for to dwell on all the face of the earth, and hath determined the times before appointed, and the bounds of their habitation. That they should seek the Lord, if haply they might feel after him and find him, though he be not very far from every one of us

THE FOLLOWING POINTS ARE CLEAR:

1st.—All nations were from one source.

2d.—By God's decree they were to inhabit "All the face of of the earth."

3d.—Their distribution as to "times" and "bounds" God directs.

4th —"They should seek the Lord," he would not command them to seek unless it were possible that he should be found. Peter said, "Of a truth I perceive that God is no respecter of persons, but in every nation he that feareth him and worketh righteousness is accepted with him."—Acts 10: 34.

As the nations of the eastern continent sought and found God, and had revelation and covenant relation with him, so could the nations of the western continent, in fulfillment of God's covenant to Abraham. "And in thy seed shall all the nations of the earth be blessed, because thou hast obeyed my voice."—Gen. 22: 18. The Prophet Ezekiel, in chapter 37, mentions two "sticks," [records], one for Judah and the children of Israel his companions, "another stick [record] for Joseph and for all the house of Israel, his companions."

The stick for Judah being the Bible, a similar record or "another stick" should appear for Joseph. This is realized in the Book of Mormon, which is a record of the dealings of God with the descendants of Joseph on the western continent. It is therefore of equal authority with other sacred writings, and throws light upon doctrine, promise and prophecy. For as Paul says, "All scripture is given by inspiration of God and is profitable for doctrine, for reproof, for correction, for instruction in righteousness, that the man of God may be thoroughly furnished in all good works.—2 Tim. 3:16. It does not in any sense supplant the Bible or take its place, but is a companion volume thereto.

CHAPTER III.
THE JAREDITES FROM BABEL.

On pages 501–2, (new edition 445–6) of the Book of Mormon is an account of the Jaredites who were led from the tower of Babel to a "choice land," "beyond the sea." In answer to prayer they were permitted to retain their language, which was the Adamic, and so were not given a new language in the confusion of tongues. The statement found in Gen. 9:18, 19, confirms such position: "And of them [sons of Noah] was the whole earth overspread." The foregoing declaration was evidently intended to include in its fulfillment, events connected with the confusion of tongues at Babel. It is written: "So the Lord scattered them abroad from thence upon the face of all the earth. Therefore is the name of it called Babel; because the Lord did there confound the language of all the earth, and from thence did the Lord scatter them abroad upon the face of all the earth."—Gen 11:8, 9.

Opinions of many old Spanish writers were expressed in substance by Father Duran in 1585 in his history, "New Spain." "Adair the expert, and Emanuel De Moraes, agree that the Quichees by tradition affirm that they made a long journey by land and crossed the sea from the east. The tradition of their origin states that they came from the far east across immense tracts of land and water."

It is scarcely presumable that from the year 1492 A. D. to the year 1585 A. D., only 93 years having elapsed, that the Indians could have had such a tradition created and received among them as coming down through their sages, by their limited contact with the treacherous Spaniards, who had from the very beginning betrayed all confidence reposed in them.

"The most ancient civilization on this continent, judging from the combined testimony of tradition, records, and architectural remains, was that which grew up under the favorable climate and geographical surroundings which the Central American region southward of the Isthmus of Tehuantepec afforded. The great Maya family with its numerous branches, each in time developing its own dialect, if not its own peculiar language, at an early date fixed itself in the fertile valley of the river Usumasinta, and produced a civilization which was old and ripe when the Toltecs came in contact with it. Here in this picturesque valley region in Tabasco and Chiapas, we may look for the cradle of American civilization. Under the shadow of the magnificent and mysterious ruins of Palenque a people grew to power, who spread into Guatemala and Honduras, northward toward Anahuac and southward into Yucatan, and for a period of, probably twenty-five centuries, exercised a sway, which at one time, excited the envy and fear of its neighbors

"We are fully aware of the uncertainty which attaches itself to tradition in general, and of the caution with which it should be accepted in treating of the foundation of history; but still, with reference to the origin and growth of old world nations, nothing better offers itself in many instances than suspicious legends. The Histories of the Egyptians, the Trogens, the Greeks, and even of ancient Rome rests on no surer footing. Clavigero says, the Chiapanese have been the first peop'ers of the new world, if we give credit to their traditions. They say that Votan, the grandson of that respectable old man that built the great ark to save himself and family from the deluge, and one of those who undertook the building of that lofty edifice, which was to reach up to heaven, went by express command of the Lord to people that land.

"The tradition of Votan, the founder of Maya culture, though somewhat warped, probably by having passed through priestly hands, is nevertheless one of the most valuable pieces of information which we have concerning the Ancient Americans. Without it our knowledge of the Mayas would be a hopeless blank and the ruins of Palenque would be more a mystery than ever.

"According to this tradition, Votan came from the East, from Valum Chivim, by the way of Valum Votan, from across the sea, by divine command, to apportion the land of the new continent to seven families which he brought with him."—North Americans of Antiquity, John T. Short, pages 203-4.

Short says, of Francisco Nunes de la Vega, Bishop of Chiapas, who had read a book or document discovered by him and which is mentioned as a Votanic document, "He fails to give any definite information from the document except the most general statements with reference to Votan's place in the calendar, and his having seen the Tower of Babel, at which each people was given a new language."—Ibid 206. "While some of the details of Votanic tradition are not worthy of a moments consideration, it is quite certain that in the general facts we have a key to the origin of what all Americanists agree in pronouncing the oldest civilization on this continent, one which was already gray and declining when the Toltecs entered Mexico. There is not the slightest evidence that it originated in any other place than in Chiapas where it is found, and extended itself into Guatamala, Yucatan, and probably branched northward in a colony as remote as Culhuacan."—Ibid 210.

It is found in the history of the Toltecs that this age and first world, as they call it, lasted 1716 years: that men were destroyed by tremendous rains and lightnings from the sky, and even all the land, without the exception of anything, and the highest mountains were covered up and submerged in water * * fifteen cubits * * and how after men multiplied they erected a very high * * tower * * in order to take refuge in it, should the second world [age] be destroyed Presently the language was confused, and not able to understand each other, they went to different parts of the earth. The Toltecs, consisting of seven friends and their wives, who understood the same language, came to these parts. * * 520 years after the flood."—Ibid 238.

In the introduction to his History General, (Sahagun) in speaking of the origin of this people, expresses the opinion that it is impossible to definitely determine more than that they report, "That all the natives came from seven caves, and that these seven caves are the seven ships or galleys in which the first populators of the land came. This people came in quest of the terrestial paradise, and were known by the name of Tamoanchan, by which they mean, "We seek our home."—Ibid 242.

All of the above citations are very confirmatory of the account cited in the Book of Mormon, respecting the migration of the Jaredites to the western continent. As to the peculiar construction of the vessels of the Jaredite colony, (which are eight in number, seven of which were used for the people, the remaining one specially for their cargo), the following is very interesting: "The little steamer Norton, which is to sail from Long Island Sound for Southern France to-morrow, is, it is claimed by her builder and captain, a craft that cannot sink. She is only 58 feet in length, but the most conspicuous feature about her is that she has a double bottom and six ballast compartments. Water is admitted through HOLES IN THE OUTER BOTTOM. When the boat careens, the body of water between the bottoms presses the air in the compartments and acts as a ballast, the air serving as a cushion. This prevents the boat from capsizing or from diverging far from its center, even in the roughest seas. It is claimed that the double bottom and air tight compartments make it impossible to sink should the boat be cut in two. If the builder's theory be correct, its application will revolutionize naval architecture. The result of the Norton's first voyage will be awaited with great interest."
—Philadelphia Record, Dec. 13. 1891.

"If Victor Hugo were now alive he would have a new field, or new light on one of his old fields of work. Navigating the sea has always been supposed to mean

plowing the surface, whatever the motor might be.
But we can now travel under the sea as well as on the
surface. Recent experiments have been made at Toulon with a submarine boat, that proves to be a great
success. It runs from nine to ten knots, while the
light is good and respiration easy. The boat can be
moved in any direction, either vertically or horizontally. It will carry five persons. Of course its purport
is warfare, but there is no reason why such a boat may
not be applied to purposes more peaceful, especially to
aid scientific research."—Globe Democrat, February
3d, 1889.

CHAPTER IV.

TWO DISTINCT AND HIGHLY CIVILIZED PEOPLES.

"The Neolithic and Bronze ages preceded the Paleaolithic at least in the Mississippi Basin, not that the
last inhabitants deteriorated and lost the high arts
which are well known to have been cultivated upon the
same soil by them, but that they were preceded by a
race possessed of no inferior civilization, who were not
their ancestors, but a distinct people with a capacity
for progress, for the exercise of government, for the
erection of magnificent architectural monuments, and
possessed of a respectable knowledge of geometrical
principles."—North Americans of Antiquity, (Short),
page 27.

Pidgeon says: "From these facts in connection
with the traditions of De Coo Dah respecting the ancient inhabitants of these regions, as of various lan-

guages, customs and color, we are led to the conclusion that at least TWO DISTINCT RACES of men have occupied this territory at different eras, and that both became nationally extinct anterior to the occupation of the present Indian race."—Traditions of De Coo Dah, pp. 176-7.

Bancroft says: "The resemblance in the different groups of ruins in Chiapas, Yucatan and Honduras, are more than sufficient to prove intimate connection between the builders. The differences pointed out prove just as conclusively that the edifices were not all erected and dedicated by the same people, under the same laws and religious control, at the same epoch."—Native Races, Pacific States, Vol. 5, p. 259.

We have now presented Short, Pidgeon and Brancroft; three eminent authorities, on there having been two distinct peoples, and who preceded the aborigines of America, in the possession of this land, which supports the claim of the Book of Mormon for the Jaredite and Nephite colonizations. These three authorities agreeing as to the "two distinct" peoples, and Mr. Short classing them as having "capacity" for the "exercise of government," "erection of magnificent architectural monuments," and possessed of a "respectable knowledge of geometrical principles," we shall now present evidences of high civilization without classification.

Pidgeon says: "It cannot any longer be denied that there has been a day when this continent swarmed with millions of inhabitants, when the arts and sciences flourished."—Antiquarian Researches, p. 5.

Of ancient American's knowledge of astronomy, Donnely says: "It will be conceded, that a considerable degree of astronomical knowledge must have been necessary to reach conclusively that the true year consisted of 365 days and six hours; (modern science has demonstrated that it consists of 365 days, five hours, less ten seconds) and a high degree of civilization was requisite to insist that the year must be brought around by the intercalation of a certain number of days in a certain period of time, to its true relation to the season. Both were the outgrowth of a vast ancient civilization of the highest order."—Atlantis, p. 368.

Le Plongeon says: "The Troano, (Maya Book) is a very ancient treatise on Geology."—Sacred Mysteries, page 78. So it will certainly appear that at that day the science of Geology was not without its devotees and propagators in ancient America. Of "Chimu," a city of South America built by the ancients, Donnely says: 'Tombs, temples and palaces arise on every hand, ruined but still traceable, immense pyramidal structures, some of them a half mile in circuit; vast areas shut in by massive walls, each containing its water tank, its shops, municipal edifices, and the dwellings of its inhabitants, each a branch of larger organization; prisons, furnaces for smelting metals, and almost every concomitant of civilization existed in the ancient Chimu Capital."—Atlantis, p. 393.

- Baldwin says: "To find the chief seats and most abundant remains of the most remarkable civilization of this old American race, we go into Central America and Mexico. Many ancient cities have been discovered. * * The chief peculiarity of these ruins, is the evidence they furnish that their builders had remarkable skill in architecture and * * ornamentation. * *

The rooms and corridors in these edifices were finely and often elaborately finished; plaster, stucco, and sculpture being used. "Throughout," he again says, (quoting Stephens), "The laying and polishing of the stones are as perfect as under the rules of the best modern masonry. The ornamentation is no less remarkable than the masonry and architectural finish "—Ancient America, pp. 93, 99.

The Marquis de Nadillac, author of Prehistoric America, says of the old civilization of Peru: "Nowhere in the world perhaps has man displayed greater energy. It was in these desolate regions that arose the most powerful and most highly civilized empire of the two Americas, * * imposing ruins, * * fortresses defending it, * * roads intersecting it, * * canals conducting the water for fertilizing the fields, * * houses of refuge, in the mountains for the use of travelers, * * potteries, linen and cotton cloth, ornaments of gold and silver, which are sought for by the Tapadas, with insatiable zeal."—Prehistoric America, p. 388.

Speaking of the ruins of Pa'enque, Mr. Short says: "Of 'stucco relief' that was in a 'temple there,' M. Waldec with the critical insight of an experienced artist declares it 'Worthy to be compared to the most beautiful works of the age of Augustus '"—North Americans of Antiquity, (Short), p. 387.

William Hoséa Ballou, in Scientific American for January 26th, 1889, quoting Le Plongeon, says: "Here (at Chichen) were many beautiful mineral paintings, probably the only vestiges now existing of ancient American art."

With regard to the calendar stone of Mexico, Bancroft says: "The calendar stone was a rectuangular parallelopipedo, of porphyry, 13 feet, 1½ inches thick, and weighing in its present state 24 tons The concentric circles, the divisions, and the subdivisions, without numbers are traced with mathmatical exactitude ".— Native Races, Vol. 4, pp. 506-8.

Thus it will be seen that these various authors clearly and distinctly affirm that the ancient denizens of America possessed high culture, polish and civilization. And so do they add their testimony in support of the Book of Mormon, for that is in line with its statements touching these things.

CHAPTER V.

BOOKS, WEAVING AND DYEING.

Elder Wm. Woodhead in writing for Herald says: "The following description of the 'Troano' will probably be a fair one, as to the merit of the 'many ancient Maya books said to have been destroyed by the vandalism of Landa and other early fathers.' 'The Troano,' says Dr. L. Plongeon, 'is a very ancient treatise on geology."—Sacred Mysteries, p. 70.

Of writing in Central America, Baldwin says: "The ruins show that they had the art of writing, and that at the south this art was more developed, more like a phon-tic system of writing than that found in use among the Aztecs." "It is known that books or manuscript writings were abundant among them in the ages previous to the Aztec period."—Ancient America, p. 187

It is evident then that these books were not the fruits of association with the Spaniards, for the Aztec period antedated the Spaniards by some centuries.

Elder R. M. Elvin, contributing to the Herald, wrote: "One of the offices among the ancient people was to write history and chronicle events."

Baldwin says: "These chroniclers had likewise to calculate the days, months and years, and though they had no writings like ours, they had their symbols and characters through which they understood everything, and they had great books, which were composed with such ingenuity and art, that our characters were really of no great assistance to them. Our priests have seen those books, and I myself, * * many were burned at the instigation of the monks. * * Books, such as those here described by Las Cassas must have contained important historical information."—Ancient America, p. 18. Again: "We learn from Spanish writers that a still greater destruction of the old books was affected by the more ignorant and fanatical of the Spanish priests who were established in the country as missionaries after the conquest. This is said by Las Cassas, himself, one of the missionaries "—Ibid 189.

"In Peru a paper was made of plantain leaves, and books were common in the earlier ages."—Atlantis, p. 451.

"Some of the Peruvian tongues had names for paper, and according to Montesino's writing, and books were common in the older times, that is to say, in ages long previous to the Incas."—Ibid 255.

"Humboldt mentions books of hieroglyphical writings found among the Paneoes, on the river Ucayli.

A Franciscan missionary found an old man * * reading one of these books to several young persons."—Ibid 255-6.

Boudinot says: "There is a tradition related by an aged Indian of the Stockbridge Tribe, that their fathers were once in possession of a SACRED BOOK, which was handed down from generation to generation, and at last HID IN THE EARTH, since which time they have been under the feet of their enemies."—American Encyclopedia, Art. Boudinot.

Baldwin says of Mound Builders: "They manufactured cloth, but their intelligence, skill and civilized ways are shown not only by their constructions and manufactures, but also by their mining works."—Ancient America, p. 61.

McLean says: "The Mound Builders * * for their principal raiment used cloth regularly spun with a uniform thread, and woven with a warp and woof. Fragments of clothing have been taken from a low mound near Charleston, Jackson county, Ohio. In constructing the Cincinnati, Hamilton and Dayton R. R. a mound was cut through near Middleton, Ohio, and in it * * was found cloth connected with tassels and ornaments."—Mound Builders, p. 73.

"The American Nations manufactured woolen and cotton goods. * * They manufactured glass, they engraved gems and precious stones."—Atlantis, p. 142.

Baldwin in speaking of the Peruvians says: "They had great proficiency in the arts of spinning, weaving and dyeing. For their cloth they used cotton and wool of four varieties of the llama, that of the vicuna being the finest. Some of their cloth had interwoven designs and ornaments very skilfully executed. * * They possessed the secret of fixing the dye of all colors, flesh-color, yellow, gray, blue, green, black, etc , so firmly in the thread, or in the cloth already woven, that they never faded during the lapse of ages, even when exposed to the air, or buried (in tombs) under ground. Only the cotton became slightly discolored, while the woolen fabrics preserved their primitive lustre. It is a circumstance worth remarking that chemical analyses made of pieces of cloth of all the different dyes prove that the Peruvians extracted all their colors from the vegetable and none from the mineral kingdom In fact, the natives of the Peruvian mountains now use plants unknown to Europeans, producing from them bright and lasting colors."—Ancient America, pp. 247–8

I give one citation of many in the Book of Mormon which are amply sustained by the above mentioned authorities: "Behold their women did toil and spin and did make all manner of cloth of fine twined linen, and cloth of every kind."—Plano Edition, Book of Mormon, p. 394. New Edition, p. 348, v. 11½.

CHAPTER VI.

ISRAEL IN AMERICA.

That Israel was to be scattered far wider than the eastern continent, is evident from Isaiah 11: 11, 12. "And it shall come to pass that the Lord shall set his hand again the second time to recover the remnant of his people which shall be left, from Assyria, and from

Egypt, and from Pathros, and from Cush, and from Elam, and from Shinar, and from Hammath, and from the islands of the sea. And he shall set up an ensign for the nations and assemble the outcasts of Israel, and gather the dispersed of Judah from the four corners of the earth."

The liberal mention of lands, supplemented by "and from the islands of the sea," covers all lands in its scope. The "ensign for the nations," and to "assemble the outcasts of Israel, and gather together the dispersed of Judah, from the four corners of the earth," contemplates the entire earth. The effort to "recover" outcast Israel and dispersed Judah must occur after the year 70 A. D., when Judah was "dispersed" and Jerusalem destroyed.

The first desolation and scattering of Israel occurred about 590 B. C. when the power of Babylon wrought the complete overthrow of the Jews, and destroyed Jerusalem and burned the magnificent temple erected by Solomon.

The first restoration occurred about 520 B. C. when their beloved Jerusalem was restored, and the temple rebuilt, under the splendid patronage and aid of Cyrus, king of Persia, the great ruler of the east.

The second desolation and scattering came in the year 70 of the Christian era; when the famed city, "beautiful for situation," and "the joy of the whole earth," was laid in ruins, and the second temple razed to the ground: when the Jews perished by pestilence, famine and war; and only a remnant escaped, to endure exile and captivity under the yoke of the Roman Empire.

The second restoration, which is so plainly predicted by the prophet, can only occur after the second scattering and exile of that people; and therefore, must have its fulfillment subsequent to the year 70 of the Christian era.

The Prophet Amos said: "And I will plant them upon their own land, and they shall no more be pulled up out of their land, which I have given them, saith the Lord thy God."—Amos 9: 15.

"My sheep wandered through all the mountains, and upon every high hill: yea, my flock was scattered upon all the face of the earth, and none did search or seek after them. For thus saith the Lord God: Behold, I, even I, will both search my sheep and seek them out. As a shepherd seeketh out his flock, * * so will I seek out my sheep * * out of all places. * * I will bring them out from the people, and gather them from the countries, and will bring them into their own land."—Ezek. 6: 11, 13.

The above, presents vividly, the extensive scattering of the past, and the complete gathering yet to be, and Israel being planted in "their own land" from which they were "outcast" and "dispersed." Israel here called "sheep" are so mentioned by Christ; "Go not into the way of the Gentiles, and into any city of the Samaritans enter ye not: But go rather to the lost sheep of the house of Israel."—Matt. 10: 5, 6. God, who "Hath determined the times before appointed" and the "bounds" of * * "habitation," gave the "sure word of prophecy" portraying the history of his chosen people, ere it came to pass;" and so we are enabled to trace Israel, by ancient promise and prophecy to the land of America:

Genesis 48: 11-20, relates the blessing of Joseph's sons. Manasseh and Ephriam, by Jacob; Ephriam, the younger receives the special, or "right hand" blessing, while the custom was in favor of the first born. Of the two, Jacob said, "He [Manasseh] also shall be great, but truly his younger brother shall be greater than he, and his seed shall become a multitude of nations * * and he set Ephriam before Manasseh. Genesis 49: 22-26 presents the blessings of God to Joseph's posterity. "Joseph is a fruitful bough, even a fruitful bough by a well, whose branches run over the wall. [or that surrounding that continent, the sea]· The God of thy fathers * * shall help thee, * * the Almighty * * shall bless thee with blessings of heaven above. [revelation] blessings of the deep that lieth under: blessings of the breast and of the womb. The blessings of thy father have prevailed above the blessings of my progenitors unto the utmost bound [afar off] of the everlasting hills: they shall be on the head of Joseph and on the crown of the head of him that was separated from his brethren."

The geographical extent of the lands of the progenitors of Jacob, [Abraham and Isaac] is described minutely, and nations mentioned who were occupying it. "And the Lord appeared unto Abraham and said, unto thy seed will I give this land: and there he builded an altar unto the Lord, who appeared unto him." —Gen. 13: 15. "For all the land which thou seest, to thee will I give it, and to thy seed forever."—Gen. 12: 7. "In that same day the Lord made a covenant with Abraham, saying, Unto thy seed have I given this land, from the river of Egypt unto the great river, the river

Euphrates: The Kennites, Kenizzites, * * Kadmonites, * * Hittites, Perizzites, * * Rephaim, * * Amorites, * * Cananites, Girgashites, * * and the Jebusites."—Gen. 15:18-21.

"And I will give unto thee, and to thy seed after thee, the land wherein thou art a stranger, all the land of Canaan, for an everlasting possession, and I will be their God."—Gen. 17:18.

While the above described and limited country was given to Abraham and his seed, to Joseph and his seed, God added that "over the wall, [sea] unto the utmost bounds of the everlasting hills," or those farthest away.

Deut. 33:13-17, gives a description of Joseph's land. "And of Joseph he said. blessed of the Lord be his land, for the precious things of heaven, for the dew and the deep that coucheth beneath, * * precious fruits brought forth by the sun, * * the moon, * * chief things of ancient mountains, * * precious things of the lasting hills, and for the precious things of the earth and the fulness thereof, and for the good will of him that dwelt in the bush, let the blessings come upon the head of Joseph, and upon the top of the head of him that was separated from his brethren."

The description thus given through Moses of Joseph's land must certainly apply to that land "afar off * * "the utmost bounds of the everlasting hills," and cannot describe that little strip of tribal inheritance upon the coast of the Mediteranean sea. There was nothing of special significance in the blessing of the land upon the Mediteranean, that such a glowing and enlarged statement of its luxuriance and richness should have been given. "Blessed be his [Joseph's] land for the precious things of heaven above." This we understand to be revelation from God.

Now we ask, What special blessing of God did Joseph receive in his first or tribal inheritance? We know of none. But after going over and beyond the sea, or "wall" as the prophet describes it, their record, the Book of Mormon, tells us that God in his loving kindness and eternal wisdom, gave to them the revelation of his will concerning them from time to time. The land of America will certainly do justice to the splendid description of Joseph's land given by the prophet. For this is a choice land above all other lands of the earth; varied in its richness of climate, of soil, of mineral resources, abounding in all things the heart could desire; from the ice-bound regions to those of the tropics, affording almost all the fruits of the earth. All of these things point to the Western Continent as Joseph's land. This theory is supported by the following texts: "O vine of Sibmah, I will weep for thee with the weeping of Jazer; thy plants are gone over the sea."—Jer. 48: 32. "For the fields of Heshbon languish, and the vine of Sibmah; the lords of the heathen have broken down the principal haunts thereof * * they have gone over the sea."—Isaiah 16: 18.

As identifying the "vine of Sibmah," "whose plants are gone over the sea," "For of old time have I broken thy yoke, and burst thy bands."—Jer. 2: 20. This clearly describes the freeing of Israel from Egyptian bondage, as does also: "Thou hast brought a vine out of Egypt, thou hast cast out the heathen and planted it."—Ps. 80: 8. Joseph's posterity, the "branches of the fruitful bough," which were to "run over the wall;"

the plants of the "vine of Sibmah, are, without doubt, of Israel.

Now if they went over the sea, or "wall," as the prophet termed it, where did they go? What other land save the Western-Continent alone can fulfill the terms of prophetic description, as given by Moses? We know of none. Surely it is not found in Europe, or among the nations of Asia. Here was the land, "choice above all other lands."

Besides this evidence of a portion of Israel emigrating from the eastern to the western continent, is the warning of the Prophet Jeremiah, disclosing King Nebuchadnezzar's "purpose," and the warning of God, commanding them to flee. "Flee, get you far off; dwell deep, [go secretly, unobserved], O ye inhabitants of Hazor, saith the Lord, for Nebuchadnezzar hath taken counsel against you, and hath conceived a purpose against you. Arise, get you up unto the wealthy nation, that dwelleth without care, saith the Lord, which have neither gates nor bars, which dwell alone. And their camels shall be a booty, and the multitude of their cattle a spoil, and I will scatter into all winds them that are in the utmost corners, and I will bring their calamity from all sides thereof, saith the Lord." —Jer. 49: 30–32.

The following points are prominent: First, They were to "flee;" "get you far off;" "dwell deep;" (go unobserved). Second, They were to go to a "wealthy nation that dwelleth without care," one occupying a land "alone," and, therefore, had neither "gates nor bars" to keep away others, as was the case upon the eastern continent. Third, The camels of the "wealthy nation," were to be a "booty;" "the multitude of their cattle a spoil." Fourth, Those by whom the "booty" and "the spoil" should be left, were to be "scattered to all winds," carried away, obliterated, become extinct, "them that are in the utmost corners" their "calamity" was to "come from all sides;" such was the case with the Jaredite nation in every point. They were "afar off," "wea thy," "dwelt alone," without gates or bars; having grown wicked, were in a continual war, for the last battle of which the armies were four years in gathering, and in which their extinction was accomplished. (See close of Book of Esther, Book of Mormon).

The Nephites wrote: "And we did find upon the land of promise as we journeyed in the wilderness, that there were beasts in the forest of every kind, both the cow and the ox, and the ass, and the horse, and the goat, and the wild goat, and all manner of wild animals, which were for the use of men, and we did find all manner of ore, both of gold, silver, and of copper." —Book of Mormon, p. 43; N. E. p. 37, v. 130.

When the Book of Mormon was published, the horse in particular, as also other of the domestic animals, were supposed not to have been on the Western Continent until brought by the Spaniards. "In North America * * in the Champlain period there were great elephants and mastodons, oxen, horses stags, beaver, and some edentates in quarternary North America, unsurpassed by any in the world."—Text Book of Geology, J. D. Dana, L. L. D., p. 319.

"We know that the equine type of quadrupeds existed in America from the period of the Eocene. We are in fact, acquainted with twenty-one species of horse-like animals, and the genus of true horses has been traced down to the times preceding the present." Prof. A. Winchell, Chancelor, Syracuse University, Evolution, p. 82.

Prof. Cooper, in a lecture 1875, in San Francisco, said that during the "Pliocene epoch" in California, "through the luxuriant forests roamed a llama as large as a Bactrian camel; herds of huge Buffalo disported in the meadows along with wild horses of a giant race."

Prof. Hayden in his report of "Explorations in the West," says: "Seven species of rhinoceros existed on the plains of Colorado; twenty-seven species of horses also cropped the herbage of those vast savannas, varying in size from that of our domestic variety, down to that of a New Foundland dog."

The Book of Mormon mentions two large, very large animals, classing them with the elephant. The statement as found in Chambers' Encyclopedia, Vol. 6, Art. Mastodon, is therefore full of significance: "Eleven or twelve species have been described from the Miocene, Pliocene and Pleistocene strata in Europe, Asia and America."

Of the third and smaller number of people who migrated to the western continent, it is recorded on page 137, (N. E., p. 121) Book of Mormon, that they came from Jerusalem when Zedekiah, who was afterward carried captive into Babylon, was king of Judah. Of this people the Prophet Ezekiel says: "Thus saith the Lord God; I will also take the highest branch of the high cedar, and will set it; I will crop off from the top of his young twigs a tender one, and will plant it upon a high mountain and eminent: In the mountain

of the height of Israel will I plant it; and it shall bring
forth boughs, and bear fruit, and be a goodly cedar;
and under it shall dwell all fowl of every wing; in the
shadow of the branches thereof shall they dwell."—
Ezek. 17: 22. 23.

First, King Zedekiah was of Israel. Second, Those
taken from his household were to be planted in the
"mountain of the height of Israel," where a government
would arise in which could "dwell" all "fowl of every
wing," or men from all the races, as is the case in
America.

The Prophet Isaiah, describes in a graphic manner
the Western Continent: "Wo to the land shadowing
with wings, which is beyond the rivers of Ethiopia."—
Isaiah 18: 1.

First, The American continent is in the form of a
pair of wings. Second, It lies west, or beyond the
rivers of Ethiopia, from where the prophet had his
abode, at Jerusalem.

Zephaniah 3: 10, "From beyond the rivers of
Ethiopia my suppliants, even the daughters of my dispersed, shall bring mine offering." This text presents
the people of the western land, or that land "beyond
the rivers of Ethiopia," bringing offering, which supports all that is claimed in the foregoing chapter in regard to the location of Israel.

For Joseph, whose posterity was to come to the
Western Continent, as hitherto shown, there was to be
a record. "The word of the Lord came again unto
me, saying, Moreover, thou son of man, take thee one
stick, and write upon it for Judah, and for the children
of Israel his companions: then take another stick, and

write upon it, For Joseph, the stick of Ephriam, and for all the house of Israel his companions: And join them one to another into one stick; and they shall become one in thine hand. And when the children of thy people shall speak unto thee, saying, Wilt thou not show us what thou meanest by these? Say unto them, Thus saith the Lord God; Behold, I will take the stick of Joseph, which is in the hand of Ephraim, and the tribes of Israel his fellows, and will put them with him, even with the stick of Judah, and make them one stick, and they shall be one in mine hand."—Ezek. 37: 15-19.

First, There is to be a stick (record) for "Judah" and "Israel his companions." Second, "Another stick" (record) for "Joseph in the hand of Ephriam, and Israel his companions." Third, They are to be joined "one to another," and thus made companion volumes. Fourth, God was to put the stick (record) in the hand of Ephriam with that of Judah, which, in the preservation of the records of the Book of Mormon and their translation was fulfilled. Fifth, Ephriam's pre-eminence as shown in his blessing, is clearly brought to light, in his possession of the "stick of Joseph," and "Joseph's land." The Western Continent is therefore provided with its record, as was the eastern, with the record of God's dealings with His people upon that land.

The prophet says: "I have written to him the great things of my law, but they were accounted as a strange thing"—Hosea 8: 12.

CHAPTER VII.

HEBREW RELICS, CUSTOMS AND LANGUAGE IN AMERICA.

Bancroft says: "The theory that the Americans are of Jewish descent has been discussed more minutely and at greater length than any other. Its advocates, or at least those of them who have made original researches, are comparatively few, but the extent of their investigations and the multitude of parallelisms they adduce in support of their hypothesis exceed by far any thing that we have yet encountered "—Native Races, Vol. 5, pp. 77-8.

Joseph Merrick, Esq., gave the following account, that in 1815 he was leveling ground, situated on Indian Hill, * * discovered a black strap, threw it into an old tool box, * * later found it, * * was formed of two thick pieces of raw hide, sewed and made water tight, with sinews of some animal and gummed over * * in the fold was contained four pieces of parchment. They were of a dark yellow hue and contained some kind of writing. The neighbors tore one of the pieces to atoms * * the other three pieces Mr Merrick saved and sent them to Cambridge where they were examined and discovered to have been written by a pen in Hebrew, plain and legible. The writing was quotations from the Old Testament. See American Ant., pp. 68-70.

Mr. A. A. Bancroft thus describes a relic: A "slab of stone of hard and fine quality, an inch and a half thick, eight inches long, four and a half inches wide at one end, and tapering to three at the other. Upon the face of the slab was the figure of a man, apparently a priest, with a flowing beard, and a robe reaching to his feet; over his head was a curved line of characters, and upon the edge and back of the stone were closely and neatly carved letters. The slab which I saw myself, was shown to the Episcopalian clergyman of Newark, and he pronounced the writing to be the Ten Commandments in ancient Hebrew."—Antiquities of Licking Co., Ohio.

The following is a representation of the supposed "key stone," found 29th of June, 1860, (near Newark, Ohio, by D. Myrick): "This stone is in the shape and size represented by the cuts, and has upon each of the four sides a Hebrew inscription in the Hebrew character, which when translated reads: 'The King of the earth;' 'The word of the Lord;' 'The laws of Jehovah;' 'The Holy of Holies.' Another stone, "Encased in a stone box buried some twenty feet in the earth * * was found on the 1st of November, 1851, has 'four cuts' on its 'four sides,' * * with the characters on each side, the English of which appears to be an abridgement of the Ten Commandments. The translation was given by J. W. McCarty. The word "Moses" and the statement "Who brought them them out of the land of Egypt," * * appears above an image on the stone."—Traditions of De Coo Dah, pp. 116, 117.

Of four stones and Rev. Miller's lecture on relics found in Ohio, Elder Josiah Ells of Pittsburgh. Pa., wrote to the Herald in 1866, the following: "Rev. R. M Miller, lecturing in the First Presbyterian church, Alleghany, Pa., on relics found near Newark, Ohio, containing Hebrew inscriptions, exhibited a photograph of a stone head, on the forehead of which was written in Hebrew, 'May the Lord have mercy on an untimely birth.' The original was owned by Mr. Tenant of Newark, Ohio Another relic owned by Mr. Strock, of Newark, contained in Hebrew: 'It is good to love the aged;' and, 'The heart is deceitful.' A third relic, in the shape of a wedge, had on its respective four sides in Hebrew: 'The Lord is King of all the earth;' 'The sword of the Lord is the law;' 'The Holy of Holies;' 'The jew of life is the Lord awakening souls.' A fourth called a Teraphim or household god by Mr. Miller, (he quoted Judges 17th chapter to prove it), was eight inches long, three wide and two thick, having a depression on one side half an inch deep, in which was carved a figure of a man dressed in priestly robes, over t e head the word Moses, on the back and edges was the Ten Commandments. This Teraphim was found by digging into a very large mound, two and a half miles from Newark, Ohio, at some depth, and in a stone box in 1860, and was owned by David Johnson of Coshocton, Ohio.

"The Rev. Miller seemed a good Hebrew scholar as he read and criticised the language in the presence of several of the theological professors of the Presbyterian college of Alleghany City. He stated that he had shown them to several learned Rabbis, and they were agreed that the Hebrew characters were of a date beyond Ezra.

"Mr. Miller described on a black-board, the difference of formation of the letters before and after that period. His conclusions were: First, That some of the tribes or parts of tribes of Israel had once inhabited this land: Second, That they were Mound Builders."

Of these stones or similar ones, "The Prophetic Watchman" of September 14th, 1866, said: "We are all more or less acquainted with the so-called 'Indian Mounds,' found in various parts of our country. * * 'For centuries it has been a most interesting subject of inquiry as to who built these mounds and whence came their builders. Within the last few years some relics have been discovered which are thought to throw light upon the subject. The first is a little coarse sand stone, not quite an inch and a half high by two inches long. It was found in the 'Wilson Mound' and bears the face of a human being. On the forehead are five distinct Hebrew characters, which are interpreted to mean "May the Lord have mercy on him (or me) an untimely birth," evidently an expression of humiliation. The second relic from the same mound is a stone closely resembling lime stone. It is rather triangular than square, in its form, and yet differs widely from both. It represents an animal, and contains four human faces and three inscriptions in Hebrew, signifying devotion, reverence and natural depravity. The third stone was found in 1860, about three miles from Newark. It is shaped like a wedge and is about six inches long, tapering at the end. On one end is a handle and at the top are four Hebrew inscriptions The last relic is an object of much interest; it was found in 1860 and has engraved upon it Moses and the Ten Commandments. One side is depressed and the reverse protudes. Over the figure is a Hebrew word signifyig Moses. The other inscriptions are almost literally the words found in some parts of the Bible, and the Ten Commandments are given in part and entirely, the longest being abbreviated. The alphabet used, it is thought, is the original Hebrew one, as there are letters not known in the Hebrew alphabet now in use, but bearing a resemblance to them. All things on this stone point to the time BEFORE Ezra."

G. R. Lederer, editor "Israelite Indeed," wrote in May, 1861: "We suppose that many if not most of our readers have seen in religious, as well as in secular papers, the accounts of some relics which were found a.few months ago in a mound near Newark, Ohio. These relics consist of stones of strange shapes, bearing Hebrew inscriptions, which makes the case particularly interesting to me as a Hebrew." "In calling a few days ago on my friend, Mr. Theodore Dwight (the Recording Secretary of the American Ethnological Society and my associate in the editorship of this magazine) my eyes met with the very object of my desire. That I examined these antiquities carefully none of our readers will, I think, entertain any doubt. I recognized all the letters, except one, (the ayin) though the forms of many of them are different from those now in use."

According to the statement of the Book of Mormon, that portion of Israel known as the Nephites and Lamanites came over to the Western Continent about

600 B. C. Usher's chronology locates Ezra's prophecy, ending 556 B. C. It would be of the current Hebrew in its letters and forms of the TIMES OF EZRA, that the Nephites would have brought with them. The fact that the Hebrew discovered upon the relics already described, is clearly of that period, is a strong proof in support of the claim made in the Book of Mormon. This is the stronger, when it is known that since A. D. 1829, the searcher and seeker after the curious of antiquity have been at work, constantly increasing the volume and variety of evidence, all in confirmation of the testimony of this book

Of the Indians, Priest says: "Their Jewish customs are too many to be enumerated in this work Hebrew words are found among the American Indians in considerable variety."—American Antiquities, pp. 56, 63.

Prescott says: "When the Indians make, their feasts they remove all fire, * * and rekindle it before the food is put on to cook, so as to be sure and not have anything unclean about the feast. For my part I am forced to believe that these feasts have been handed down from the children of Israel."—Ibid 241.

Palacio relates that at Azori in Honduras, the natives circumcised boys before an idol called Icelca."—Carta, p. 84.

Mahenda and Acosta affirm that the southern Indians observed a jubilee year according to Israel's usage." Boudinot, p. 250.

Acosta says: "That the South American Indians dress like the ancient Jews, that they wear a square little poke over a little coat."

M. Edwards in his history of the West Indies says: "The striking conformity of prejudices and customs of the Charivee Indians to the practice of the Jews has not escaped the notice of historians, as Gamella and Du Terte and others."—Ibid 250.

Dr. Beattie in Beattie's Journal says, of a visit he paid the Indians on the Ohio about the year 1770, that an old Christian Indian informed him that an old uncle who had died about 1728, related to him several customs and traditions of former times; and among them that circumcision was practiced among the Indians long ago, but their young. making mock of it, brought it into disrepute, and so it came to be dismissed. The Indians to the eastward say that in Central and eastern America, previous to the white people coming into the country, their ancestors were used to the custom of circumcision, but latterly not being able to assign any reason for so strange a practice, their young people insisted upon it being absolved. See Boudinot 113.

"Souard, in his Melenges De Litera¹ure, or literary miscellany, speaking of the Indians of Guiana says, on the authority of a learned Jew, Isaac Nasic, residing at Suriam, that the language of the Indians, which he calls the Galobe dialect, says, it is soft and agreeable to the ear, abounding in vowels and synonyms, and possessing a syntax as regular as it would have been had it been established by some academy. This Jew asserts that all the substantives are Hebrew. The word expressive of soul in each language means breath. They have the same word in Hebrew to denominate God, which means Master or Lord."—Ibid 107.

Lact, in his description of South America, says: That he had often heard the Indians repeat the word "Hallelujah;" others attest that "Jehovah" or "Yehova" is found in frequent use. Ibid 107.

H. A. Stebbins reported for the Herald: "A learned Indian lecturing in Wisconsin in 1868 said that 500 Indian words within his knowledge were Hebrew

A table of words and phrases is furnished by Dr. Boudinot, Adair and others, to show the similarity, in some of the Indian languages, to the Hebrew, and that the former must have been derived from the latter. The following is an example afforded from the sources quoted:

WORDS.

ENGLISH.	INDIAN.	HEBRAIC, OR CHALDAIC.
Jehovah,	Yohewah,	Jahoveh,
God,	Ale,	Ale, Aleim.
Jah,	Yah or Wah,	Jah.
Shiloah,	Shilu,	Shiloh.
Heavens,	Chemim,	Shemim.
Father,	Abba,	Abba.
Man,	Ish, Ishie,	Ish.
Woman,	Ishto,	Ishto.
Wife,	Awah,	Ewah, Eve.
Thou,	Keah,	Ka.
His wife,	Liani,	Lihene.
This man,	Uwoh,	Huah.
Nose,	Nichiri,	Neheri.
Roof of a house	Taubana-ora,	Debonaou.
Winter,	Kora,	Korah.
Canaan,	Canaai,	Canaan.

THE BOOK UNSEALED. 35.

To pay,	Phale,	Phalace.
Now,	Na,	Na.
Hind part,	Kesh,	Kish.
Do,	Jennais.	Jannon.
To blow,	Phaubac,	Phauhe.
Rushing wind....	Rowah,	Ruach.
Ararat, or high mt.	Ararat,	Ararat.
Assembly,	Kurbet,	Grabit.
My skin,	Nora,	Ourni.
Man of God, ...	Ashto Allo,	Ishda Alloa.
Waiter of the high priest.	Sagan,	Sagan.

PARTS OF SENTENCES.

ENGLISH.	INDIAN.	HEBREW.
Very hot,	Heru hara or hala,	Hara hara,
Praise to the first cause.	Hallehuwah,	Hallelujah.
Give me food,	Natoni boman,	Natoni bamen.
Go thy way,	Bayon boorkaa,	Bona bonak.
Good be with you,	Halea tibon,	Ye hali etonboa.
My necklace,	Yene Kali,	Vongali.
I am sick,	Nane guale,	Nance heti.

Boudinot further says: "Their languages in their roots, idioms and particular construction, appear to have the whole geinus of the Hebrew; and what is very remarkable, have most of the peculiarities of that language, especially those in which it differs from most other languages."—The American Indians, pp. 98-101.

In regard to the ruins of Palenque, Stephens says: "The intermediate country is now occupied by races of Indians speaking many different languages and entirely unitelligible to each other; but there is room for the belief that the whole of this country was once occupied by the same race, speaking the same language, or at least having the same written characters."—Travels in Central America, Chiapas and Yucatan, Vol. 2, p. 343.

CHAPTER VIII.

EGYPTIAN RESEMBLANCE AND LANGUAGE IN AMERICA.

Of Moses it is said: "And Moses was learned in all the wisdom of the Egyptians and was mighty in words and deeds."—Acts 7:22. He was also supposed to have entered the Egyptian priesthood, as was the custom for kings' sons, except those who were enthroned."—Fragmental History, Vol. 2, p. 580.

It will be remembered that during Joseph's sojourn in Egypt, he became distinguished in learning, as no doubt others did during those times. The contact of the children of Israel with the Egyptians for hundreds of years, during which time flourished a Joseph and a Moses, skilled in all the learning of that renowned land, and the services of Moses as their instructor for forty years, would certainly be sufficient to establish Egyptian customs and language with that people. And if Israel came to America, we may reasonably look for and expect Egyptian traces and resemblances in America.

Delafield says: "On a review then of the architectural evidence, we trace identity between the Mexicans and Peruvians and the Egyptians, in (First) the coincidence in the pyramidal sarcophagi and temples, and their peculiar structure. (Second.) The possession of the same architectural and mechanical genius which enabled them to remove masses, which our mechanical ski l has not attained to. (Third.) The peculiarity of hieroglyphic inscription of the zodiac and planispheric sculpture in their sacred buildings. (Fourth.). An identity of architectural and sepulchral decorations. (Fifth.) An analogous construction of bridges. (Sixth.) A singular analogy in the specimen given of their sculpture "—Delafield, p 61.

Bancroft says: "Resemblances have been found between the calendar systems of Egypt and America, based chiefly upon the length and division of the year, and the number of intercalery and complimentary days."—Native Races, Vol. 5, p. 62.

Pidgeon says: "Ancient Egypt, first in science and famous in art, has also left her impress here. In 1775 some of the first settlers in Kentucky, whose curiosity was excited by something remarkable in the arrangement of stones that filled the entrance to a cave, removed them, and on entering, discovered a number of mummies, preserved by the art of embalming in as great a state of perfection as was known by the ancient Egyptians 1800 years before Christ; which was about the time the Israelites were in bondage in Egypt. This custom would seem as purely Egyptian, and was practiced in the earliest age of their national existence. A trait of national practice so strong and palpable as is this peculiar art, should lead the mind without hesitation to the belief that wherever it was practiced, its authors or pupils existed."—Traditions of De Coo Dah, p. 19.

"As to the Mexicans it would be superfluous to examine how they obtained their knowledge. Such a problem would not soon be solved; but the fact that the intercalation of 13 days in every cycle, that is, the use of a solar year of $365\frac{1}{4}$ days, is proof that it is either borrowed from the Egyptians, or that they had a common origin."—Delafield, p 53.

Elder R M. Elvin in writing for Herald, says: "Wm. Hosea Ballou in the Scientific American of January 6th, 1889, gives the following statement from Dr. Le Plongeon, 'Here (Uxmal) were many beautiful mineral paintings, probably the only vestiges now existing by ancient American art. * * They were on the walls, which were smoothly and beautifully plastered The paintings were in vegetable colors the same as upon the tombs of Egypt. They represent the history of the life of the individual buried beneath the mansoleum.'"

Bancroft says: "The colums of Copan stand detached and solitary, so do the obelisks of Egypt, both are square or four sided and covered with sculpture." —Native Races, Vol. 5, p. 60.

"Strange indeed that even the obelisks of Egypt have their counterpart in America. Molina, in his history of Chilli says: 'Between the hills of Mendoza and La Punta is a pillar of stone 150 feet high and 12 feet in diameter.'"—History of Chilli, tom. 1, p. 169.

The report of the Davenport Academy of Science for 1882, in the description of the stone tablet says: "This tablet, * * represents a planetary configuration, the twelve signs of the Zodiac known to all nations of old. and seven planets conjoined with six different signs. * * The figures of the signs are the same which we find depicted on Egyptian, Greek, Roman and other monuments."—Presidency and Priesthood, p. 286.

"There is a very distinct resemblance in some of these hieroglyphics (of Central America) to those of Egypt."—Prehistoric America, p. 328

"Above the door and simulating windows, (in the valley of Youcay, one of the tributaries of the Amazon), we meet again with the Egyptain 'tau' that we have already seen at Palenque"—Ibid, p. 417.

"The ornamentations of the buildings resemble that upon Egyptian monuments."—Ibid, p. 324.

"Statues resemble those of Egypt and head dress a little like that of the Assyrians."—Ibid, p. 327.

"They wore a head dress that has been pronounced Egyptian."—Ibid, p. 392.

As to the hieroglyphical writing, Delafield says: "Their buildings, particularly the sacred houses, were covered with hieroglyphics Each race, Egyptian, Mexican and Peruvian recorded the deeds of their gods upon the walls of their temples."—Inq. Origin Am. Ant., p 60.

Wm. Woodhead contributing to Herald writes: "The shape of the temples" (in Yucatan and Central America) "was that of the Egyptian letter **M**, called ma ▭, a word that also means "place," "country" and, by extension, "the Universe." The Egyptians adopted it, therefore, not because they believed, as Dr. Fanton suggests, that the earth was square or oblong; for they knew full well it was spherical, but because the sign of the word "ma" conveyed to their mind the idea of the earth, as the word "earth" represents it to ours. But ma is also the radical of Mayax; and likewise, in the Maya language, it means "the country," "the earth."—Sacred Mysteries, p. 33.

Again he says, concerning prehistoric man in Central America: "In all the buildings, whatever their size, the ground plan was in the shape of an oblong square, ▭, that is of their letter **M**, pronounced ma. Ma is the contraction of Mam, the ancestor, as they denominated the Earth, and by extension the Universe. Ma is also the radical of Mayax, the name of the Yucatan peninsula, in ancient times. * * * in Egypt, and in Mayax the figure ▭ in the hieroglyphics, stands for Earth and Universe."—Ibid, p. 62.

▭ "It is the letter **M**, pronounced Ma. of the Maya and Egyptian ancient alphabets. It is the radical of Mayax, name of the empire; but Ma in Egypt as in Mayax, is a word that signifies country, and by extension, Universe; and in Mayax as in Egypt ▭ is one of the signs for land."—Ibid, p. 104.

Now this is curious enough, ain't it, that a people that sixty years ago were said to have been nearly savages with "no mental culture or intellectual development," should be now found to represent the earth by the same hieroglyphic that the enlightened Egyptians did. Both nations represented the earth by the same sign, and it is remarkable, too, that the same sign should not only be the same in form, but also the same in meaning in both countries, in their hieroglyphics and alphabets! The sign ▭ "conveyed to their minds the idea of the earth, as the word 'earth' represents it to ours," and did not mean to them an earth with four corners; "they knew full well it was spherical." The fact is, "they knew the rotundity of the earth, which it was supposed Columbus had discovered." See Atlantis, p. 364.

The Nephites engraving their plates in reformed Egyptian, is not a strange claim, in the light of their association with Egyptian learning in the times past.

CHAPTER IX.

PLATES—RECORDS.

Elder J. R. Lambert in the Independent Patriot says: In the days of Job writing on imperishable material was understood. Job 19:23, 24: "Oh that my words were now written! oh that they were printed in a book! That they were graven with an iron pen and lead in the rock forever"

It was understood and practiced in the days of Moses. Exodus 39:30: "And they made the plate of the holy crown of pure gold, and wrote upon it a writing. like to the engravings of a signet, Holiness to the Lord."

In the Apochrypha, 1 Mach. 14:48, 49, we have the following plain statements: "And they commanded that this writing should be put in tables of brass, and that they should be set up within the compass of the sanctuary, in a conspicuous place: and that a copy thereof should be put in the treasury, that Simon and his sons may have it.'"—Douay Translation.

"After the destruction of Jerusalem, about A. D. 70, Titus, the Roman general, called at Antioch, and the people presented to him a petition against the Jews. Of this translation Josephus says: 'Whereupon the people of Antioch, when they had failed òf success in this their first request, made him a second; for they desired that he would order those tables of brass to be removed, on which the Jews' privileges were engraven,' etc."—Josephus, vol. 6, p. 132.

The American nations writing on metal plates and other imperishable materials, is not strange in the light of this, and is highly probable in the case of the Nephites, as they were Israelites.

The claim of the Book of Mormon that the ancient American nations had written on metalic plates, was thought to be its sure defeat; but plates and various materials containing hieroglyphical writing have since been found in such abundance, that the claim is now fully sustained.

In the Quincy (Ill) Whig appeared an article describing plates found April 23d, 1843:

"A Mr. J. Roberts from Pike county, called upon us last Monday with a written description of a discovery which was recently made near Kinderhook in that county. * * It appeared that a young man by the name of Wiley, a resident of Kinderhook, commenced digging into a mound, finding it quite laborious, he invited others to assist him; finally a company of ten or twelve repaired to the mound and assisted. * * After penetrating the mound about eleven feet they came to a bed of limestone that had been apparently subjected to the fire. They removed the stones * * to the depth of two feet, * * when they found six brass plates secured or fastened together by two iron wires, but which were so decayed that they readily crumbled to dust upon being handled. The plates were so completely covered with rust as almost to obliterate the characters inscribed upon them, but after undergoing a chemical process, the inscriptions were brought out plain and distinct. There were six plates four inches in length, 1¾ inches wide at the top, and 2¾ wide at the bottom, flaring at the points. There are four lines of characters or hieroglyphics on each * * In the place where the plates were deposited, were also found human bones, in the last stage of decomposition; * * it is believed that it was but the burial place of a small number, perhaps a person or a family of distinction, in ages long gone by, * * of a people that existed far, far beyond the memory of the present race. * * The plates, above alluded to were exhibited in this city last week."

Wiley and eight others testify to the finding of these plates in the "Times and Seasons," as follows: "We the citizens of Kinderhook, whose names are annexed, do certify and declare that on the 23d of April, 1843, while excavating a large mound in this vicinity, Mr. Wiley took from said mound six brass plates of a bell shape, covered with ancient characters. Said plates were very much oxidated. The bands and rings on said plates mouldered into dust on a slight pressure. R. Wiley, George Deckenson. W. Longnecker, G. W. F. Ward, J. R. Sharp, Ira S. Curtiss, Fayette Grubb, W. P. Harris, W. Fugate."

G. W. West of Manchester, Adams county, Ohio, wrote an article dated January 19th, 1880, which appeared in Herald, in which it is set forth that, Near Manchester, Adams county, Ohio, on the old Smith farm on the Portsmouth pike, in 1880, in a cave where twenty-five bodies had been entombed as in Egypt, was found a square package at the head of a tomb, wrapped in varnished cloth containing A BOOK of 100 leaves of thin COPPER, fastened loosely at the top and crowded with finely engraved characters. Mr. Samuel Groom, who owned the farm at the time, is reported as having forwarded these to the Smithsonian Institute.

Elder R. M Elvin contributed to the Herald as follows: "The Newport, Vermont, Express and Standard of August 15th, 1882, quoting from the New Orleans Democrat says: "The pyramids and mounds which so often occur in the western states * * have been leveled * * by zealous searchers for relics of antiquity. Nor have their efforts been in vain, copper hatchets, chisels and various other kinds of tools have been unearthed with copper plates covered with inscriptions."

In the St. Louis Chronicle in February, 1889, appeared the following: "Rev. S. D. Peet, the well known antiquarian, is reported as having found in Illinois two cross plates which have all the appearance of being rude musical instruments. These plates are about fifteen inches square and there are places for strings and a bridge. Along the lower edge is a row of hieroglyphics SIMILAR to those on the famous Palmyra plates, said to have been discovered by Joseph Smith and from which he interpreted the Book of Mormon."

John T. Short on pages 38-9 of North Americans of Antiquity, describes two tablets and presents a cut of one, found near Davenport, Iowa, of which he says: "The most remarkable discovery of all, however, (relics of eastern Iowa) was made January 10th, 1877, by Rev. Mr. Gass, * * two tablets of coal slate covered with a variety of figures and hieroglyphics were found.

The Cincinnati tablet is described thus: "The material is a fine grained compact sandstone, of light brown color. It measures five inches in length. by three in breadth at the ends, two and six tenths at the middle, and is about half an inch in thickness. The sculptured face varies very slightly from a perfect plane. The figures are cut in low relief, (the lines being not more than one twentieth of an inch deep), and occupying a rectangular space of four inches and two tenths long, by two and one tenth wide."—Mound Builders, p. 275. This tablet was found November, 1841, corner of 5th and Mound streets, Cincinnati, Ohio.

"In 1870 there was found a tablet in a mound near Lafayette Bayou, * * Miss., which has the same reduplication of figures in the carved work as exists in the Cincinnati Tablet."—Mound Builders, p. 110.

Another, known as the Berlin tablet, found near Berlin, Ohio, by Dr. J. E. Sylvester, June 14th, 1876, described on the last page cited, is similar to the last two treated upon.

Statements concerning other plates and tablets could have been given, but the foregoing abundantly establish the claim of the Book of Mormon, as to ancient Americans having written on plates of imperishable material.

The Book of Mormon plates were found in a STONE BOX in the earth. The SAME is true of HEBREW TABLETS mentioned in chapter seven of this work.

The Davenport tablet and another plate found are described in a foot note, on page 38, of J. T. Short's work, American Antiquities, thus: "The two plates were closely encircled by a single row of weathered limestones. These stones are irregular in shape but almost of the same size, their dimensions being about 3x7 or 8 inches, and the diameter of the circle two feet

Ellen Russell Emerson says: "The Ujibway Indians, relates 'Mr. Copway,' had three depositories for sacred records near the waters of Lake Superior. Ten of the wisest and most venerable men of the nation dwelt near these, and were appointed guardians of them."—Indian Myths, pp. 225-6.

There is a tradition related by an aged Indian of the Stockbridge Tribe, that their fathers were once in possession of a SACRED BOOK, which was handed down from generation to generation, and at last HID IN THE EARTH; since which time they had been under the feet of their enemies."—American Encyclopedia Art Boudinot.

The Book of Mormon mentions coins of different value, used as money. In the light of this, the following is interesting as well as confirmatory of its statement. Correspondence to the press, from Helena, Arkansas, bearing date of October 19th, 1891, says: "A most remarkable find is reported from the little town of Laconia, about twenty-five miles south of this city. A well was being drilled, at the depth of 125 feet the drillings showed they were passing through a layer of brick. * * As there were no brick houses in the town and never had been it could not be believed. While quite a crowd was around the well-hole, the men brought up to the surface a lot of mud and examined it, as they had done from the time they found the brick residue. In the mass of mud there was a small piece

of metal, which when cleaned off, was found to be a PIECE OF MONEY. It was octagonal in shape and had hieroglyphics on it, which could not be deciphered, but which were evidently meant to represent the value of the piece. * * It is claimed by antiquarians here that the bricks and COIN are the relics of a prehistoric race which lived here many years before the Indians, and built the pavements and roads which were discovered at Memphis, on the other side of the river above here."
—Zion's Ensign, Nov. 21st, 1891.

"A round copper COIN with a serpent stamped on it was found at Palenque, and T shaped copper coins are very abundant in the ruins of Central America."—Atlantis, p. 245.

CHAPTER X.
METALS, IMPLEMENTS AND INSTRUMENTS.

The Book of Mormon on pages 43, 64, 394, and 520 (N. E. pp. 38, 348, 462) as also elsewhere, mentions gold, silver, brass, copper, steel and iron. The ancient Americans were supposed to have used stone for tools; but not the several precious metals; and for years the Book of Mormon was alone in this claim, for the use of metals on the western continent.

"The Peruvians had such immense numbers of vessels, and ornaments of gold that the Inca paid with them a ransom for himself to Pizzaro of the value of fifteen million dollars."—Atlantis, p. 142.

"The Peruvians called gold, 'The tears wept by the sun.' * * The great temple of the sun at Cuzco was

called the 'Place of Gold.' It was as I have shown literally a mine of gold. Walls, cornices, statuary, plate, ornaments, all were of gold; the very sewers, pipes and aqueducts, even the agricultural implements used in the garden of the temple were of gold and silver. The value of the jewels which adorned the temple, was equal to one hundred and eighty millions of dollars."
—Atlantis, pp. 344–5.

In speaking of Costa Rica, Mr. Bancroft says: "Mr. Boyle makes the general statement that gold ornaments and idols are constantly found, and that the ancient mines which supplied the precious metal are often seen by modern prospectors."—Native Races, Pac. States, vol. 4, p. 23.

Mr. Squire says: "These articles have been critically examined and it is beyond doubt that the copper bosses were absolutely plated, not simply overlaid with silver. Between the copper and the silver exists a connection such as it seems to me could only be produced by heat, and if it is admitted that these are genuine relics of the Mound Builders, it must at the same time be admitted they possessed the difficult art of plating one metal upon another."—Atlantis, pp. 376–8.

Priest says: "In many instances articles made of copper and sometimes plated with silver have been met with on opening their (Mound Builders) works."—Inquiry Origin American Ant., p. 256

"In South America * * many interesting specimens have been exhumed. * * 'Among these,' says Dr. Reese, 'are mirrors of various dimensions of hard shining stones, highly polished, * * hatchets and other instruments, * * some were of flint, some of copper, hardened by an unknown process to such a degree as to supply the place of iron."—Mayers Mexico, p 227.

Bryant describes copper instruments found in Wisconsin: "An adze with wings for fitting. An arrow head with wings for fitting to arrow. A knife with socket for handle. A chisel apparently cast, the roughness showing sand-mould, and white spots of melted silver. An awl. A spear head, 11 inches in length, with socket for handle."--History U. S., vol. 1, p. 31.

Of discoveries at Circleville, Ohio, Priest says: "On this mirror was a plate of IRON which had become an oxide; but before it was disturbed by the spade, resembled a plate of CAST IRON "—Priest's Am. Ant., pp. 178-9. The size of mirror mentioned is given as one and a half by three feet.

But besides this, there have been found very well manufactured swords and knives of IRON and possibly STEEL, says Mr. Atwater."—Ibid, p. 259.

"It is remarkable," says Molina, "that iron which has been thought unknown to the ancient Americans, had particular names in some of their tongues. In official Peruvian it was called, quillary; and in Chilian, panillac. The Mound Builders fashioned implements out of meteoric iron."—Foster's Prehistoric Races, p. 333, (Atlantis, 451.)

Again he says: "We found the remains of an iron sword and meteoric weapons in the mounds of the Mississippi Valley, while the name of the metal is found in the ancient languages of Peru and Chili, and the Incas worked in IRON on the shores of Lake Titicaca."—Ibid. p. 462.

Priest says: "In Virginia, near Blacksburg, eighty miles from Marietta, there was found the half of a STEEL BOW, which when entire would have measured five or six feet."—Priest's American Antiquities, p. 176.

Jones says: "In 1834, Coles, Meriwether and Lumsden, while engaged in digging a canal in Dukes Creek Valley, Georgia, * * unearthed a subterraneous village * * of thirty-four small cabins. They were made of logs hewn at the ends and notched down. * * This hewing and notching had evidently been done with sharp metallic tools, the marks being such as would have been caused by a chopping axe. * * Eleven old shafts have been found varying in depth from 90 to 100 feet. In 1854 one * * was cleaned out, * * at 90 feet was found a windlass of post-oak well hewn, with an inch auger hole through each end. Distinct traces where it had been banded with iron. * * The presence of iron and the marks of sharp metallic tools prove that these ancient mining operations cannot be referred to the labor of the Indians "—Antiquity of Southern Indians, pp. 48–9.

"The American nations built public works as great or greater than any known in Europe. * * Humbolt pronounces these Peruvian roads, 'among the most useful and stupendous works ever executed by man. They built aqueducts for purposes of irrigation, some of which were 500 miles long. They constructed magnificent bridges of stone, and had even invented suspension bridges thousands of years before they were introduced into Europe. They had, both in Peru and Mexico, a system of posts, by means of which news was transmitted hundreds of miles in a day."—Atlantis, p. 141–2.

THE GREAT PERUVIAN ROADS.

"Nothing in ancient Peru was more remarkable than the public roads. No ancient people has left traces of works more astonishing than these, so vast was their extent, and so great the skill and labor required to construct them. One of these roads ran along the mountains through the whole length of the empire, from Quito to Chili. Another, starting from Cuzco, went down to the coast and extended northward to the equator. These roads were built on beds or deep under-structures of masonry. The width of the roadways varied from twenty to twenty-five feet, and they were made level and smooth by paving, and in some places by a sort of macadamizing with pulverized stone mixed with lime and bituminous cement. This cement was used in all the masonry. On each side of the roadway was a very strong wall more than a fathom in thickness. These road went over marshes, rivers, and great chasms of the sierras, and through rocky precipices and mountain-sides. The great road passing along the mountains was a marvelous work. In many places its way was cut through rock for leagues. Great ravines were filled up with solid masonry. Rivers were crossed by means of a curious kind of suspension bridges, and no obstruction was encountered which the builders did not overcome. The builders of our Pacific Railroad, with their superior engineering skill and mechanical appliances, might reasonably shrink from the cost and the difficulties of such a work as this. Extending from one degree north of Quito to Cuzco, and from Cuzco to Chili, it was quite as long as the two Pacific railroads, and its wild route among the mountains was far more difficult. * * Along these roads at equal distances were edifices, a kind of caravanseras, built of hewn stone, for the accomodation of travelers "—Baldwin's Ancient America, pp. 243, 244–5.

Of the metals mentioned at the opening of this chapter, brass is the only one not supported by evidence in this chapter. In the last chapter the reader will remember it is shown that the KINDERHOOK PLATES ARE BRASS

The class of works found in chapter four, setting forth clearly the civilizations of ancient America, together with the stupendous works named in this chapter, especially the great Peruvian roads, will convince reasonable minds that the metals, and especially STEEL, was in common use. To grant that such tasks were performed without it, would be to admit for those ancient workmen far more skill than if they possessed it.

Since the confusion of Babel was followed by the scattering of man from "Thence upon the face of all the earth," (Gen. 11:8) and as a knowledge of metals must then have obtained in order to the building of the ark, there is no reason why the knowledge of the metals may not have been brought to the western continent by its first inhabitants.

Wilkinson says: "Iron and copper mines are found in the Egyptian desert which were worked in old times, and monument of Thebes and even their tombs about Memphis, dating more than four thousand years ago, represent butchers sharpening their knives on a round bar of metal, attached to their aprons, which from its blue color can only be STEEL; and the distinction between the bronzed and iron weapons in the tomb of Ramases III, one painted red and the other blue, leaves no doubt of both having been used (as in Rome) at the same period."—American Encyclopedia, vol. 9, p. 389.

The Nephites used a compass or instrument similar to it, as recorded in the Book of Mormon. Of the compass, Donelly says: "In A. D. 868 it was employed by the Northmen." (The Landnamabok, vol. 1, chap. 2.)

An Italian poem of A D. 1190, referred to it as in use among the Italian sailors at that date. In the ancient language of the Hindoos, the Sanscrit, which has been a dead language for a period of 2200 years, the magnet was called "The precious stone beloved of iron." The Talmud speaks of it as "The stone of attraction," and it is alluded to in the early Hebrew prayers as "kalamitah," the name given it by the Greeks, from the reed upon which the compass floated.

In the year 2700 B. C. the Emperor (of China) Wangti, placed a magnetic figure with an extended arm, like the Astarte of the Phœnicians, on the front of carriages, the arm always turning and pointing to the south, which the Chinese regarded as the principal pole."—Atlantis, pp. 440-1.

The Chinese invented the mariners compass eleven centuries before Christ. See Light in Darkness, by J. E. & A. H. Godbey, p. 289.

CHAPTER XI.
DATES OF AMERICAN ANTIQUITIES. WHEN PUBLISHED.

As to whether or not it was possible for Joseph Smith to have read works of antiquity, and then have written the Book of Mormon in conformity with the findings of the explorers, the following is very interesting: Bancroft writes, "Since 1830 the veil has been lifted from the principal ruins of ancient Maya works, by the researches of Zalva, Waldec, Stephens, Cartherwood, Norman, Fredderickstahl and Charney. A general account of the antiquarian writings and explorations of these gentlemen is given in the appended note,—It will be noticed that all the authors mentioned who write from actual observation, have confined their observations to from one to four of the principal ruins, whose existence was known previous to their visits, excepting Messrs. Stephens and Cartherwood. These gentlemen boldly left the beaten track and brought to the knowledge of the world about forty ruined cities, whose very existence had been previously UNKNOWN even to the residents of the larger cities of the very state in whose territory they lie." "The visit of these explorers was the first, and thus far proved in most cases, the last."— Native races, vol. 4, pp. 144-46.

Baldwin says of Central America: "Palacios, who described Copan in 1576, may properly be called the first explorer."—Ancient America, p. 102.

The discovery by Palacios was not published however until 1843, and not in English until 1860. See

Native races, vol. 4, page 79, also American Encyclopedia, Article Squier

In his "Origin American Antiquities," published in 1839, Delafield says: "The antiquities of America are an immense field hardly entered, abounding in promise of reward for the most devoted investigations."

Priest says in his book of 1833: "It yet remains for America to awake her story from its oblivious sleep, and tell the tale of her antiquities, the traits of nations, coeval perhaps, with the oldest works of man this side of the flood."

Bancroft writes: "The only author who has attempted to treat of the subject of Central American Civilization, and antiquity comprehensively as a whole, is the Abbe Brasseur de Bourbourg."—Native Races, vol- 2, p. 116. The work cited was first published in 1857-9 See American Encyclopedia, vol. 3, p. 214.

He further writes: "Of all American peoples, the Quichees of Gautemala have left us the richest mythological legacy. Their description of the creation as given in the Popol Vuh, which may be called the national book of the Quichees, in its rude, strange eloquence and poetic originality, one of the rarest relics of aboriginal thought. In Vienna in 1857, the book, now best known as the Popol Vuh, was FIRST brought to the notice of European Scholars."—Native Races, vol. 3, p. 42.

The Book of Mormon was published in 1830, and so gave the facts twenty-seven years BEFORE this last mentioned publication.

Bancroft writes: "For what is known of Copan, the world is indebted almost entirely to the works of the American traveler, Mr. John L. Stephens, and of his most skilfull artist companion, Mr. F. Cartherwood."—Native Races, vol. 4, p. 81.

These gentlemen were sent out in 1839 by the United States government. Mr. Stephens wrote. "I shall make one remark in regard to the work of Mr. Waldec, which was published in folio in Paris in 1845, and except my own hurried notice, is the ONLY ACCOUNT that has ever been published of the ruins of Uxmal."—Incidents of Travel, vol. 1, p. 297.

CHAPTER XII.

JOSEPH SMITH'S OBJECT—A VISION.

My object in going to inquire of the Lord, was to know which of all these sects was right, that I might know which to join * * I asked the personages, who stood above me in the light, which of all the sects was right,—for at that time it had never entered my head that all were wrong,—and which I should join. I was answered that I should join none of them, for they were all wrong; and the personage who addressed me said that all their creeds were an abomination in his sight, that those professors were all corrupt, 'They draw near me with their lips, but their hearts are far from me;' 'They teach for doctrine the commandments of men,' 'having a form of godliness, but they deny the power thereof.' He again forbade me to join any of them."—Times and Seasons, vol. 3, p 727.

On the eve of the 21st of September, 1823, through fervent prayer, another vision was presented to Mr.

Smith, and he gives it, in part, as follows: "After I had retired to my bed for the night, I betook myself to prayer and supplication to the Almighty God for forgiveness of all my sins and follies, and also for a manifestation to me, that I might know of my state and standing before him, for I had full confidence in obtaining a divine manifestation, as I had previously had one. While I was thus in the act of calling upon God, I discovered a light appearing in the room, which continued to increase until the room was lighter than at noonday, when immediately a personage appeared at my bedside, standing in the air, for his feet did not touch the floor He had on a loose robe of most exquisite whiteness It was a whiteness beyond anything earthly I had ever seen, nor do I believe that any earthly thing could be made to appear so exceedingly white and brilliant. His hands were naked, and his arms also a little above the wrists; so, also, were his feet naked, as were his legs, a little above the ankles. His head and neck were also bare. I could discover that he had no other clothing on but this robe, as it was open so that I could see into his bosom. Not only was his robe exceedingly white, but his whole person was glorious beyond description, and his countenance truly like lightning. The room was exceedingly light, but not so very bright as immediately around his person. When I first looked upon him I was afraid, but the fear soon left me. He called me by name, and said unto me, that he was a messenger sent from the presence of God to me. and that his name was Moroni; that God had a work for me to do, and that my name should be had for good and evil among all nations, kindreds and tongues; or that it should be both good and evil spoken of among all people. He said there was a book deposited, written upon gold plates, giving an account of the former inhabitants of this continent, and the source from whence they sprang. He also said that the fullness of the everlasting gospel was contained in it, as delivered by the Savior to the ancient inhabitants. Also, that there were two stones in silver bows, (and these stones, fastened to a breastplate, constituted what is called the Urim and Thummim) deposited with the plates, and the possession and use of these stones was what constituted seers in ancient or former times, and that God had prepared them for the purpose of translating the book.

"After telling me these things, he commenced quoting the prophecies of the Old Testament. He first quoted a part of the third chapter of Malachi, and he quoted, also, the fourth or last chapter of the same prophecy, though with a little variation from the way it reads in our Bible. Instead of quoting the first verse as it reads in our book, he quoted it thus: 'For behold, the day cometh, that shall burn as an oven, and all the proud, yea, and all that do wickedly, shall burn as stubble; for they that come shall burn them, saith the Lord of Hosts, that it shall leave them neither root nor branch.' And again, he quoted the fifth verse thus: 'Behold, I will reveal unto you the priesthood, by the hand of Elijah the prophet, before the coming of the great and dreadful day of the Lord.' He also quoted the next verse differently: 'And he shall plant in the hearts of the children the promises made to the fathers, and the hearts of the children shall turn to their fathers; if it were not so, the whole earth would be utterly wasted at his coming.' In addition to these, he quoted the eleventh chapter of Isaiah, saying that it was about to be fulfilled. He quoted, also, the third chapter of Acts, twenty-second and twenty-third verses, precisely as they stand in our New Testament. He said that that prophet was Christ; but the day had not yet come, when 'they who would not hear his voice should be cut off from among the people,' but soon would come. He also quoted the second chapter of Joel, from the twenty-eighth verse to the last. He also said that this was not yet fulfilled, but was soon to be. And he further stated, the fullness of the Gentiles was soon to come in. He quoted many other passages of scripture, and offered many explanations which cannot be mentioned here. Again, he told me that when I got those plates of which he had spoken,—for the time that they should be obtained was not yet fulfilled,—I should not show them to any person; neither the breastplate with the Urim and Thummim; only to those to whom I should be commanded to show them. If I did, I should be destroyed. While he was conversing with me about the plates, the vision was opened to my mind, that I could see the place where the plates were deposited, and that so clearly and distinctly that I knew the place again when I visited it."—Times and Seasons, vol. 3, p. 729.

CHAPTER XIII.

THE SEALED BOOK TO COME FORTH—FULFILLMENT OF PSALM 85 AND ISAIAH 29—PALESTINE RESTORED.

The Savior said (John 17:17), "Thy word is truth."

The Psalmist said, "I will hear what the Lord will speak, for he will speak peace unto his people."—Ps. 85:8. In verse 11 he says: "Truth shall spring out of the earth, and righteousness shall look down from heaven." Verse 12 states: "Yea, the Lord shall give that which is good; and our land shall yield her increase."

Thus it will be seen (1) that the Lord was to speak unto his people; and (2) that associated with the Lord speaking, would be the coming forth of "truth," a record of God's "word," "out of the earth;" and (3) that at that time the Lord was to bless the land of Palestine, and give his people "that which is good," and the "land," which had been under the curse of sterility, was again to become fertile as in ancient times.

That "truth" should "spring out of the earth," it was necessary that it should have been reposed to its keeping, to come forth in the due time of the Lord. The Book of Mormon is God's word, "truth," as delivered to the ancient nations of America; and in its coming forth "out of the earth," clearly fulfills this prophecy of the "sweet singer of Israel."

The prophet Isaiah, in chapter 29, begins with vivid expressions of "woe," "distress," "heaviness," and "sorrow" to "Ariel, the city where David dwelt;" and in the latter clause of verse 2, introduces that which says: "And it shall be unto me as Ariel." This that "shall be unto me as Ariel," is none other than another part of Israel, included in his prophecy, and not Jerusalem alone. In chapter 18 the prophet has described the Western continent, both as to its form and location, — "Woe to the land shadowing with wings, which is beyond the rivers of Ethiopia." "And thou shalt be brought down, and shalt speak out of the ground, and thy speech shall be low out of the dust." (29: 4). Being "brought down;" "speak out of the ground;" "and thy speech low out of the dust;" "whisper out of the dust," are strange particulars to be fulfilled in the history of the other Ariel, that people of whom the Savior spoke: "And other sheep I have which are not of this fold, [place] them also must I bring, and they shall hear my voice."—St. John 10: 16. This could only be accomplished by the coming forth of the records of a people perished from the earth. Of the people destroyed at Jerusalem, no record of which we have any knowledge, was ever deposited in the bosom of "mother earth;" and therefore, no record has ever been recovered from the earth, concerning that people and the times in which they lived. And now the time is already past for the fulfillment of this prophecy, as we shall show later on.

The Israel of the Western continent, committed their records to the earth; and that they have been brought forth, is fully attested by evidence which can never be impeached. The prophecies of David and Isaiah relate to the same subject, and are as one in their fulfillment, while Christ's definition of "truth" is brought out in bold relief.

The people of to-day, "The day of His preparation," (see Nahum 2:34), are presented with the record and history of those who in ages past, flourished upon the land "choice above all other lands." Verses 5 and 6 deal with the distress and destruction to be visited upon that people. In verses 7 and 8, the "nations" who were to be arrayed against Ariel, or "fight against Mount Zion," are represented as a hungry or thirsty man, who dreams of eating and drinking only to awaken and "Behold he is faint, and his soul hath appetite." These "nations" are estranged from God; and although they make a great show that they are on the Lord's side, and are fed with the manna from heaven, yet it is only as a dream, it is not real. A mistaken, apostate christianity has been their heritage, which will be confessed in that day yet to come. Hence, Jeremiah prophesied: "Gentiles shall come unto thee from the ends of the earth and shall say, 'Surely our fathers have inherited lies, vanity, and things wherein there is no profit.'"—16:19.

The Lord states their condition in Isaiah 29:9, as being "Drunken but not with wine, they stagger but not with strong drink." This evidently, portrays their spiritual condition, showing them to be spiritually drunk, having imbibed of false doctrine and heresies, partaking with the "great Babylon of the earth" "the wine of the wrath of her fornication." They were to be without present revelation from God; and to them there was to be "No answer from God." See also Micah 3:6, 7. The 10th verse (Isaiah 29) says: "For the Lord hath poured out upon you the spirit of deep sleep, and hath closed your eyes; the prophets and your rulers, the seers hath he covered." Truly their condition must have been deplorable, to have been described as drunken and sleepy, hungry and athirst. And yet this was to be their sad state, and serves but to illustrate the necessity of LIVING prophets, and teachers DIVINELY APPOINTED to minister the word of life unto the people. Verse 11 reads: "And the vision of all has become unto you, as the words of a book that is sealed, which men deliver to one that is learned, saying, read this I pray thee; and he saith, I cannot; for it is sealed." "The vision of all;" the writings of prophets and apostles as found in the Holy Scriptures, were to be possessed by that people, and to become unto them "as the words of a book that is sealed." They were to be without that inspiration of God (Job 32: 8) so necessary to understand the things of God, (see 1 Cor. 2: 11), and as a result were not to understand the things written.

"The vision of all," (or scripture possessed by them), being not understood, are compared unto another book, a book which they did not possess,—"The words of a book that is sealed." "These words," the prophet declares, "Men deliver unto one that is learned, saying, 'Read this I pray thee,' and he saith, I can not, for it is sealed." A transcript of the hieroglyphics of a certain part of the Book of Mormon were prepared by Joseph Smith, and sent by Martin Harris to Prof. Anthon of New York. When informed as to the manner of Joseph Smith obtaining the "book," he said, when asked to translate, "I cannot, for it is sealed."

Notice, that the "book" was not to be "delivered" "to one that is learned," but the "words," only; which was done when the transcript taken by Smith was delivered by Harris, as already described Verse 12: "And the book is delivered to him that is not learned, saying, Read this I pray thee; and he saith, I am not learned." To Joseph Smith was delivered the book; he was one "not learned" That he did have the records in his possession is attested by eight persons who saw and handled them, whose testimony as also that of three others, was published in connection with the Book of Mormon. He complained to the Lord, saying, "I am not learned,"

Verses 13 and 14: "Forasmuch as this people draw near me with their mouth, and with their lips do honor me, but have removed their heart far from me, and their fear toward me is taught by the precept of men: Therefore, behold I will proceed to do a marvelous work among this people, even a marvelous work and a wonder." It is clear that this "marvelous work" was not to be founded in the wisdom and precept of men, but in the wisdom and power of God Therofore the unlearned was selected, and to "him" "was delivered" the "book." The Lord was to do the work: and this is accomplished by bestowing upon the "one not learned," power from God, with the use of the "Urim and Thummim," to "read" the "book that is sealed."

The worship of the times when this was to transpire, is described as of the "lip," "while the heart is removed far me me." The hungry, thirsty, dreamy, drunken condition, one of "deep sleep," is still upon the "nations." Human precepts (creeds) are substituted for the doctrine of Christ. The "marvelous work and a wonder," so introduced by God in the latter days, occasions not a little wondering and marveling, that "The wisdom of the wise men shall perish, and the understanding of the prudent men shall be hid."—V 14.

And so we perceive another prophecy fulfilled. The efforts of the "wise" were to signally fail in their attempts to overthrow the work so introduced. Verses 15 and 16 are strong in condemnation of those who work in the dark, characterized as "Turning things upside down," opposing God's truth, perverting, instead of receiving the way of truth. Verse 17 is a veritable milestone, marking the fulfillment of prophecy: "It is not yet a very little while, and Lebanon shall be turned into a fruitful field, and the fruitful field shall be esteemed as a forest." Only "a little while" after the fulfillment of the things foretold, and Lebanon or Palestine "shall be turned into a fruitful field."

Although century upon century should pass, and Palestine during this time should remain under the curse of barrenness and sterility; yet when the time appointed of God should have arrived, and the "little while" elapsed, then the curse is to be removed, and the "land of promise" shall again be a "fruitful field." In 1830 the Book of Mormon was published, fulfilling the prophecy concerning the "words of the book that is sealed" being "delivered by men to one that is learned;" the book itself being delivered (not by man or men) to "one not learned," and God's "marvelous work" introduced.

Louis Van Buren wrote, only a few years ago, an account of his sojourn, and observations in Palestine: "I arrived in Indiana a few days since, from the Eastern Continent. I stopped at Joppa nearly the whole winter. For my part I was well pleased with the country. It is certainly a land of most wonderful fruitfulness, with a delightsome climate, producing everything, if properly cultivated, and from wo to three crops in a year. They have grain, fruit and vegetables all the year round; in fact I never was in such a country before. I have seen much good country in Europe and America, but none to compare with Palestine; its fruitfulness is uncommon, and the climate the most delightsome; even in winter I did not see the least sort of frost, and vegetables of every sort were growing in perfection in gardens. It is a fact that the rain and dew are restored; recently, in 1853, the former and the latter rain were restored, to the astonishment of the natives."—Louis Van Buren, Sen., Nov. 14th, A. D. 1867.

Thus it is seen that only twenty-three years had passed after the publication of the Book of Mormon before the long promised restoration came. According to Usher's Chronology, Isaiah made this prediction 2565 years before its fulfillment. This restoration of Palestine and the rebuilding of Jerusalem, was widely taught by the Latter Day Saints from the year 1830 down to the year 1853. They had faith in the immediate fulfillment of that promise, for they knew that the time was at hand. And now with pleasure they can point to the restoration and rebuilding of Jerusalem, and the events in the east which tend to push the sons of Abraham thither, and can say, "We told you so."

"It [Palestine] has the same bright sun and unclouded sky, as well as the early and latter rain, which, however, is diminished in quantity, owing to the destruction of trees."—Chambers' Encyclopedia, vol. 7, p. 11.—Palestine.

"The result of Dr. Barclay's observations is to show that the greatest fall of rain at Jerusalem in a single year was eighty-five inches, and the smallest forty-four, the mean being 51 1-6 These figures will be best appreciated by recollecting that the average rain fall at London during the whole year is only twenty-five inches, and that in the wettest parts of the country, such as Cumberland and Devon, it rarely exceeds fifty inches. As in the time of our Savior, (Luke 12:54), the rains come chiefly from the south or south-west; they commence at the end of October, or beginning of November, and continue with greater or lesser constancy till the end of February, or middle of March, and, occasionally, though rarely, till the end of April. Between April and November, there is, with the rarest exception, an uninterrupted period of fine weather, and skies without a cloud. During the summer the dews are very heavy, and often saturate the traveler's tent, as if a shower had passed over it. The nights, especially towards sunrise, are very cold, and thick fog or mists are common all over the country. Thunder storms of great violence, are frequent during the winter months." Dic. of Bible, by Wm. Smith, p. 636.—Art. Palestine.

In D. A. Randall's Hand Writing of God, page 19, occurs his introduction to Dr. Barclay of the Disciple church and missionary to the land of Palestine, and resident of Jerusalem twenty years, but resident of

Joppa at the time of Randall's visit. "The country about Joppa is certainly a most delightful one. Extensive plains covered with luxuriant vegetation stretched along the shore of the sea and far into the interior. Large orange groves were just yielding their luxuriant harvest of golden colored fruit. Such oranges I had never before seen and I had no idea that they ever grew to such a great size. The ground was dotted with flowers of every hue and the air was vocal with the music of birds."—Ibid, p. 23.

"Lydia or Ludd. It numbers about 2,000 inhabitants, and is surrounded by beautiful groves, among which may be seen the olive, fig and pomegranate, etc. —Ibid, p 24.

"Here, where we are now walking, and within the walls, are several large patches of ground upon which barley and wheat are growing. But a few weeks since the plow passed over that ground and the seed was scattered upon the furrowed soil, and close by it are great mounds of ruins covered with vegetation." (See Micah 3: 12)—Ibid, p. 60.

"This is about the closing up of the latter rains; after a few days they expect no more rain until the latter part of September or October."—Ibid, p. 261.

"The tall rank grass was waving among the stone, and the ground had been plowed to the very foundation walls, and a crop of barley was rapidly approaching harvest."—Ibid, 271.

"The Baldwin Locomotive works in Philadelphia, has received the following note from its representative in Palestine:

'Hotel Jerusalem, Jaffa, October 3d, 1890.

'Gentlemen:—I am very glad to be able to report that we made a successful trial trip of the first engine (Jaffa) to-day. All Jaffa was out to see it including the Turkish Governor and his court. It was estimated that at least 10,000 people were on the house-tops and along the line of the road, and over two-thirds of them never saw a locomotive before. Many of the Arab women moved their household effects along the line of the road several days ago, so as to be on hand when the great thing went along. Many flags were hoisted over public buildings in honor of the occasion. I got an American flag from the Consul and put it on the front bumper. The French engineers put two French flags on each corner of the cab, and we secured a Turkish one to put on the other corner of the bumper, and so we went up into town. I doubt if any other engine built by the works ever received so much attention as 8-24 D, 24, and as for me, well, I never expected people to regard me as the Arabs did to-day, and have been doing. They simply think I have been cutting and carving it out of a lot of railroad iron and boxes. They have a great respect for the French engineers, and think them very smart, but when it comes to making a machine such as they saw to-day, ''they can't do it in France, they had to send to America for a man to make it.' "—Hebrew Christian.

Joseph Smith affirmed that the angel said to him: "Jerusalem shall be inhabited as towns without walls for the multitude of men and cattle therein." Thus was fulfilled Zech. 2: 4, applying it to modern times. Those ancient walls, destroyed by the Roman armies, were never to be rebuilt. The city, rebuilt, is "without walls," just as the prophet declared it would be. Verse 18, (Isa. 29), "In that day shall the deaf hear the words of that book, and the eyes of the blind shall see out of obscurity and out of darkness." This has had its literal fulfillment, by many through the blessings of the restored gospel.

Verse 19: "The meek also shall increase their joy in the Lord, and the poor among men shall rejoice in the Holy One of Israel." With the increasing light of the latter days, and the blessings of the gospel of Christ once more among men, the "meek" may "increase their joy in the Lord," and the "poor among men rejoice" because they again have the gospel of Christ in its simplicity declared unto them, "Not in word only, but also in power, and in the Holy Ghost, and in much assurance." The 20th and 21st verses declare that the devices of the evil one shall be "brought to naught," the "scorner consumed," showing it to be a time of judgment. Verse 22d, is of a promise to the Hebrew. It is there stated that it is to be a time of returning favor for Jacob. "Jacob shall not now be ashamed, neither shall his face now wax pale." The long period of oppression, sorrow and affliction, visited upon them since their rejection of Jesus the Christ, is to be followed with a day of relaxation and liberty. Israel will once more enjoy his liberty among men, and the favor of God, ere they shall say in fulfillment of the Savior's words, "Ye shall no more see me till ye shall say, Blessed is he that cometh in the name of the Lord."

There has been a wonderful revolution of sentiment in favor of the Jews during this generation. And while all persecution has not ceased, yet so great has been its abatement, that many of that people have risen to positions of great honor and distinction, ranking among statesmen and leaders among the people. Surely the sons of Jacob are regaining favor among the nations, and this is in clear fulfillment of verse 22.

In this connection we shall mention a few of that race who have received positions of political honor and distinction.

— Disraeli, Premier of England, where, formerly, Hebrews were not permitted to own land. Solomon Hirsch was appointed minister to Turkey by President Harrison. Marcus Otterbourg, was the first American Hebrew to occupy the high office of Envoy Extraordinary and Minister Plenipotentiary, appointed by Pres. Lincoln to Mexico. Oscar S. Straus, Minister to Turkey, by Pres. Cleveland. Henry M. Phillips, one of the most distinguished members of the 35th Congress. Lewis C. Levin, who served in Congress three terms. E. B. Hart of the Congress of 1851. David Levy Youles, was for many years prior to the civil war, United States Senator from Florida. Isaac Phillips, General Appraiser of the port of New York, which position he held fifteen years, was appointed by Pres. Pierce. By appointment of Pres. Grant, Dr Herman Bendell, was Superintendant of Indian Affair, and later, was Consul to Denmark. Henry M. Hymans, Lieutenant Governor of Louisiana. A host of others occupying places of distinction in the leading nations could have been given.

The return of Israel unto God is signified in the 23d verse, (Isa. 29), "They shall sanctify my name, and sanctify the Holy One of Jacob, and shall fear the God of Israel." The last verse of the chapter is as follows: "They also that erred in spirit shall come to understanding, and they that murmured shall learn doctrine." Under the ministry of the gospel of Jesus Christ as again restored, "the marvelous work and a wonder," the power of the Holy Ghost, and the record of the word, will be ample and sufficient to "try the spirits" which are abroad in the earth; and as a result, those who have "erred" need not continue therein, for to them special help is promised. "And they that murmured shall learn doctrine." This is to be fulfilled by reason of the flood of light to be ushered in, and the dawning of the latter day glory. With the records of both Judah and Joseph in their midst, matters of doctrine will have right solution, and the "faith once delivered" will be fully established, and a people prepared to meet the Christ when he comes to reign on the earth.

CHAPTER XIV.

AN ADMISSION. WITNESSES TESTIFY.

PROF. ANTHON'S ADMISSION.

"Some years ago a plain, apparently simple hearted farmer called on me with a note from Dr. Mitchell, of our city, now dead, requesting me to decipher, if possible, a paper which the farmer would hand me, and which Dr. Mitchell confessed he had been unable to understand. When I asked the person who brought it how he obtained the writing, he gave me, as far as I now recollect [Note this language. 'As far as I now recollect'] the following account: A gold bo k consisting of a number of plates of gold fastened together in the shape of a book, by wires of the same metal, which had been dug up in the northern part of the state of New York, and along with the book an enormous pair of gold spectacles. [Urim and Thummim]. These spectacles were so large that if a person attempted to look through them, his two eyes would have to be turned toward one of the glasses merely, the spectacles in question being altogether too large for the human face. Whoever examined the plates through the spectacles was enabled to not only read them, but understand their meaning. All of this knowledge, however, was confined at that time to the young man who had the trunk containing the plates and spectacles in his sole possession. He put on the spectacles, or rather looked through one of the glasses, and deciphered the characters in the book, and having committed some of them to paper, handed copies to a person outside. This paper was in fact a singular scroll. It consisted of all kinds of crooked characters, disposed in columns, and had evidently been prepared by some person who had before him at the time a book containing various alphabets, Greek and Hebrew letters, crosses and flourishes. Roman letters inverted or placed sideways, were ranged in perpendicular columns, and the whole ended in a rude delineation of a circle, decked with various strange marks, and evidently copied after the Mexican calendar given by Humboldt "—E. D. Howe's work, p. 272.

THE TESTIMONY OF THREE WITNESSES.

Be it known unto all nations, kindreds, tongues, and people, unto whom this work shall come, that we, through the grace of God the Father, and our Lord Jesus Christ, have seen the plates which contain this record, which is a record of the people of Nephi, and also of the Lamanites, their brethren, and also of the people of Jared, who came from the tower of which hath been spoken; and we also know that they have been translated by the gift and power of God, for his voice hath declared it unto us; wherefore we know of a surety, that the work is true. And we also testify that we have seen the engravings which are upon the plates, and they have been shown unto us by the power of God, and not of man. And we declare with words of soberness, that an angel of God came down from heaven, and he brought and laid before our eyes, that we beheld and saw the plates, and the engravings thereon; and we know that it is by the grace of God the Father, and our Lord Jesus Christ, that we beheld and bare record that these things are true; and it is marvelous in our eyes, nevertheless the voice of the Lord commanded us that we should bear record of it; wherefore, to be obedient unto the commandments of God, we bear testimony of these things. And we know that if we are faithful in Christ, we shall rid our garments of the blood of all men, and be found spotless before the judgment seat of Christ, and shall dwell with him eternally in the heavens. And the honor be to the Father, and to the Son, and to the Holy Ghost, which is one God. Amen. OLIVER COWDERY,
DAVID WHITMER,
MARTIN HARRIS.

THE TESTIMONY OF EIGHT WITNESSES.

Be it known unto all nations, kindreds, tongues and people, unto whom this work shall come, that Joseph Smith, Jr., the translator of this work, has shown unto us the plates of which hath been spoken, which have the appearance of gold; and as many of the leaves as the said Smith has translated, we did handle with our hands: and we also saw the engravings thereon, all of which has the appearance of ancient work, and of curious workmanship. And this we bear record with words of soberness, that the said Smith has shown unto us, for we have seen and hefted, and know of a surety that the said Smith has got the plates of which we have spoken. And we give our names unto the world to witness unto the world that which we have seen; and we lie not, God bearing witness of it.

CHRISTIAN WHITMER,
JACOB WHITMER,
PETER WHITMER, JR.,
JOHN WHITMER,
HIRAM PAGE,
JOSEPH SMITH, SR.,
HYRUM SMITH
SAMUEL H. SMITH

DEATH OF THE THREE WITNESSES.

Oliver Cowdery died at Richmond, Missouri, March, 1850; his dying charge to David Whitmer, being, "Be true to our testimony, Brother David." This was related by Mr. Whitmer to the writer of this book, in company with Elder E. C. Briggs, in April, 1885, when visiting Mr. Whitmer.

Martid Harris died at Clarkston, Cache county, Utah, July 10th, 1871, answering the question of H. B.

Emerson of New Richmond, Ohio, "Did you go to England to lecture against Mormonism," said, I answer emphatically, No; I did not; no man ever heard me in any way deny the truth of the Book of Mormon " He requested a copy of the book to be placed in his hand when his death should take place —Herald.

David Whitmer died at Richmond, Missouri, where he had lived HALF A CENTURY, January 25th, 1888. Of his death and the avowal of his testimony at that time, the Richmond Democrat of January 26th, 1888, said: "On Sunday evening at 5: 30, January 22d, 1888, Mr. Whitmer called his family and some friends to his bedside, and addressing himself to the attending physician, said, 'Dr. Buchanan, I want you to say whether or not, I am in my right mind, before I give my dying testimony.' The doctor answered, 'Yes, you are in your right mind, for I have just had a conversation with you ' He then addressed himself to all around his bed-side in these words, "Now you must all be faithful in Christ; I want to say to all of you that the Bible, and the record of the Nephites (Book of Mormon) is true, so you can say that you have heard me bear my testimony on my death-bed."

The Globe-Democrat of January 25th, 1888, states of Mr. Whitmer's death: "A night or two since he called his physician, Dr. Buchanan, to his side and told him that his testimony as recorded in the Book of Mormon was true."

"We the undersigned citizens of Richmond, Ray county, Missouri, where David Whitmer, Sr., has resided since the year A. D. 1838, certify that we have been long and intimately acquainted with him and know him to be a man of the highest integrity, and of undoubted trut and veracity: A. W. Doniphan; G. W. Dunn, Judge of the Fifth Judicial Circuit; T. D. Woodson, President of Ray Co· Savings Bank; J. T. Child, Editor of Conservator; H. C. Garner, Cashier of Ray County Savings Bank; W. A. Holman, County Treasurer; J. S. Hughes, Banker; James Hughes, Banker; D. P. Whitmer, Attorney at Law; Jas. W. Black, Attorney at Law; L. C. Cantwell, Postmaster; Geo. I Wasson, Mayor; Jas. A. Davis, County Collector; C J. Hughes, Probate Judge and Presiding Justice of Ray County Court; George W. Trigg, County Clerk; W. W. Mosby, M. D ; Thos McGinnis, ex-Sherriff Ray County; J. P. Quesenberry, Merchant; W. R. Holman, Furniture Merchant; Lewis Slaughter, Recorder of Deeds; Geo. W. Buchanan, M D.; A. K. Reyburn. Given at Richmond, Mo., this March 19th, A. D. 1881.

CHAPTER XV.

CONCLUSIONS.

Now, dear reader, we solicit your candid attention, while we proceed with our statement of conclusions upon some of the many evidences presented in this work.

At the time of the coming forth of the Book of Mormon very little was known of American antiquities; but since then, interest has been awakened and effort stimulated, which have resulted in a flood of light being thrown upon the great past of ancient America. The treasure-house has been unlocked, and the remains and monuments of her ancient civilizations now tell the story of those past ages.

The students of American antiquities will find upon a careful examination that no discovery has thus far been made which in a single instance contradicts the record of America's great and glorious past, as found in the Book of Mormon

The Book of Mormon contains the record of a people who came to the Western continent from the tower of Babel at the confusion of tongues. Fortunately for the believers in the authority of the Bible, there is in the book of Genesis an historical statement which fully warrants the statement of the Book of Mormon. See Gen. 11:9.

The labors of the student of ethnology and aboriginal traditions, have resulted in finding the statements, both of Genesis and the Book of Mormon, confirmed by the clearly defined traditions of the aborigines of the Central American states. This corroboration of history and tradition, especially where the existence of one had nothing to do with the creation of the other, is but a link in the chain of facts with which the Book of Mormon is vindicated.

The Book of Mormon affirms that two Hebraic colonies came to America from Jerusalem about 600 years before the Christian era. Its statement is also in harmony with special promises and prophecies delivered by the olden Israelitish prophets concerning the colonization of a distant land by a portion of the house of Israel. (See Gen. 49:22–26; Zeph. 3:10). In this case also, now that the record attests the fulfillment of those prophetic promises made to ancient Israel, we have ample vindication of that Spirit which gave the "sure word of prophecy" unto His people in all the ages The a tiquarian comes to the front confirming the statement of prophecy, and the book which is the subject of this work We are confronted with the indisputable evidence of the Hebrew language, as found upon tablets discovered in mounds and tumuli where they were deposited in the ages long ago. Tablets and ancient parchment containing parts of the Jewish scriptures and Mosaic Law have been found, which confirm the statement of the Book of Mormon, that there was an Hebrew colonization, and that they brought their customs and religion, and also their sacred books with them when coming to this land. In this we have a striking fulfillment of ancient prophecy, and a strong endorsement of the book which records its fulfillment. The use of stone tablets and parchment for the purposes of record are of ancient custom with Israel; and their discovery in America, employing the language and the religion of that people, are strong evidences that their authors were of Israel; just as stated in the Book of Mormon.

The writers of the Book of Mormon affirm that they made records upon metalic shee s or plates, as is instanced in the golden plates from which the book itself was translated. At the time of the publication of that book there had been no discovery of an ancient writing upon a metallic sheet or plate in all America, save that alone made by Joseph Smith concerning the plates of the Book of Mormon. The wise and learned scouted the idea, not supposing for a moment that time in its developments would confirm the statements of the unlearned Smith, and the record of the Book of Mormon. And yet in the order of events calculated alike to confound the unbelieving scoffer and to inspire faith in those who accepted that book as containing a true record, only thirteen years elapsed before the discovery of what are known as the Kinderhook plates. They were of brass and covered with hieroglyphics. Only a few years ago there was a remarkable find in Ohio, when a large number of copper plates were unearthed, and these also were covered with hieroglyphical characters. And only about twenty years ago there were found in old Mexico quite a number of earthenware plates also covered with engravings. And it would seem that the work of exploration proceeds while stimulated by the thirst for discovery by those engaged in it, the providence of "Him who doeth all things well," is appropriating their labors to confirm the claims of the book, now unsealed. In this last cited proof we have a clear case in confirmation of the Book of Mormon

That book of ancient story affirms the ancient existence and use of domestic animals, such as the horse and the ox, upon the American continent. In 1830, when that publication first appeared, the idea of the horse or the ox having existed upon this land anciently was considered by men of education and learning, as simply ridiculous; for it was believed that such animals were first introduced by the Europeans after the year 1492. But in this particular, as also in others, the antiquarian serenely put in an appearance and gives a good eye-opener, effectually exploding the popular error, and fully establishing the fact that the domestic animals named, did flourish in the ages long ago upon the American continent. Thus we perceive that the wisdom of the wise, when contradicting the Book of Mormon, is brought to naught, while the statements of that book are corroborated and sustained as the years roll by. The Book of Mormon clearly affirms that in the bye-gone ages there were two distinct civilizations upon this land. And now after sixty-two years have passed since the first publications of that work, and during which time, the work of exploration has been pushed by hundreds and thousands of able men, the conclusion generally reached is that in the ages past there were two distinct peoples and civilizations upon the American continent. And so it is, that as knowledge increases and the curtain of the past is lifted and the remains of the great past are exposed to view, that one by one the statements of the Book of Mormon are verified and proven to be true.

It has ever been the privilege of God's people to have their prayers, when made in righteousess, heard and answered by the giver of all good. In this is the unchangeable character of God asserted. and His people are furnished a basis upon which to exercise faith in His word. If the ancient people of America were favored of God, and records were kept among them of their experiences from time to time, it is not unreasonable that some of their records, under divine providence, should be preserved for the enlightenment and blessing of mankind. A revelation such as the Book of Mormon claims to be, is neither unreasonable nor unscriptural, but as shown in these pages, it is both reasonable and scriptural, and therefore it is worthy of our belief.

In its fulfillment of the 29th chapter of Isaiah, the Book of Mormon has as clear a case in vindication of prophecy as was ever known among men Even those remarkable prophecies detailing the events in the life of the great Nazarene are not more lucid and explicit than are those of Isaiah 29 and Psalms 85, in their application to the coming forth of a record of truth—a book to be unsealed. The 37th chapter of Ezekiel is full of significance, pointing to the coming of another record, "The Stick of Joseph," and its being ' joined" in its use with the "Stick of Judah." The Book of Mormon alone fulfills the express terms of prophecy concerning the "sealed book" and the prophecies we have cited, and so stands as a strong witness attesting the divinity of those ancient prophecies.

It will doubtless be asked: What benefit to the believer in Christ is the book of Mormon? We answer: 1st, It gives additional witness concerning Jesus the Christ: 2d, It speaks in great plainness upon doctrine, forever setting at rest matters of doctrine in dispute among the various sects of Christendom. 3d, It contains many "precious promises" unto God's people; and like "All scripture, is given by inspiration of God, and is profitable for doctrine, for reproof, for correction, for instruction in righteousness, That the man of God may be perfect, thoroughly furnished unto all good works."—2 Tim. 3:16, 17.

We now invite attention to the witnesses whose testimony is published in the Book of Mormon which they gave to the world concerning the plates from which the book was translated, and the visitation of the angel of God who affirmed that the record so translated was true. The testimony of eight persons who saw and handled the plates while they were yet in the possession of the one who translated them, has never been impeached. Those men while they lived, constantly re-affirmed their original testimony. Their lives gave evidence of their sincerity which must be regarded as the test of truth, and all died in the faith of the Book of Mormon.

The testimony of the three special witnesses, namely: Oliver Cowdery, Martin Harris and David Whitmer, is of great significance in its relation to the coming forth of the book so attested They testify, 1st, That an holy angel brought unto them the plates of the Book of Mormon, and permitted them to handle them and see them. 2nd, That the angel bore testimony identifying the plates as those from which the Book of Mormon had been translated, and certified to the correctness and truth of the translation so made. Upon an examination of the Book of Mormon it is found that it contains a prophecy concerning this occurrence,—the testimony of the three witnesses.—See Book of Mormon page 100. Joseph Smith had also received an especial revelation in which it was asserted that the Lord would raise up three witnesses to whom would be shown those plates in a most remarkable way.—See Doc and Cov. page 69. The testimony of these men not only attests the truthfulness of the Book of Mormon, but also furnishes a most signal ins ance in the fulfillment of prophecy. In the year 1838 there was an estrangement between the three witnesses and the prophet, and under the pressure of the fiery trial and bitter persecution visited upon the Saints, these men ceased to hold membership in the church, and remained aloof during the remainder of the prophet's life. It certainly is most reasonable, that if there had been a collusion between these men to give false testimony to the world concerning the angel's testimony and the plates of the Book of Mormon, that when they ceased to be friends, and these witnesses were no more members of the church, they would have renounced their testimony, and have pronounced Joseph Smith to have been only a scheming impostor. It is, however, notorious that during their long and eventful lives, these men ever declared that Joseph Smith was a true prophet, and that their testimony concerning the Book of Mormon was true. They had affirmed an occurrence—a fact; and the years that followed furnished conclusive evidence that they were sincere in the testimony so given to the world. As men of sound minds, if they were sincere in their statement of the alleged fact, and their statements all agree, the conclusion is inevitable, that they told the truth. Upon their death-beds, they re-affirmed their testimo y, and passed peacefully away.

Coincident with the publication of the Book of Mormon was the founding anew of the church afterward known as the church of Jesus Christ of Latter Day Saints. The authority to preach the gospel and administer its ordinances had been restored to the earth, and as a result, the church with the gifts and blessings as of old, was again among men. Tongues, prophecy, interpretation of tongues, healings, and other gifts named in the 12th chapter of 1st Corinthians, were among the blessed experiences of the faithful and true of "like precious faith." Experiences and scenes like those of the day of Pentecost, are testified of by men and women from all parts of the earth. This universal testimony and witness of the Holy Ghost are surely the seal of the Almighty to the divinity of the Book of Mormon and the church of the last days. The restoration of the "former and latter rain" to the land of Palestine, just as predicted by the Prince-Prophet of Israel, coming as it does in the time of the coming forth of the "sealed book," now that the book is unsealed and published to the nations, and the "Marvelous work and a wonder" established among men, shows quite conclusively that the time is fulfilled, and the events foretold have truly come to pass.

In doctrine and promise, the Book of Mormon is in harmony with all other authoritative declarations of "law and testimony," and therefore, as tried by the divine standard, stands approved. In James 1.5, is a choice promise to those who will seek the Lord for guidance and light. In the Book of Mormon, on page 544, is a promise fraught with importance to those who love the Lord and his truth. It is there promised that if the people to whom the Book of Mormon should go, will seek the Lord for witness and testimony concerning it, that God will hear them and the Holy Ghost WILL ATTEST ITS TRUTH. Dear reader, will you not accept this TEST, and so "PROVE ALL THINGS AND HOLD FAST TO THAT WHICH IS GOOD?"

May the loving Father bless you in your search for truth, and ultimately grant you "abundant entrance" into the mansions of everlasting rest.

THE END

www.ingramcontent.com/pod-product-compliance
Lightning Source LLC
Chambersburg PA
CBHW020301090426
42735CB00009B/1171